DRUM MASTERY

A Complete Guide
for Essential Basic Techniques
and Pro Precision Exercises

MUSIC MASTERY SERIES, VOLUME 4

I0520252

By Tad Sisler

This book is dedicated to my children - Regina, Kevin, Rachel and Tad. You are the rhythm that drives my soul, the steady beat of my heart that echoes like the pulse of a drum. Your love, energy, and spirit keep my life in perfect time. This book is for you, my inspiration and my heartbeat.

TABLE OF CONTENTS: PAGE

FOREWORD

My mother, **Elaine Witt Sisler**, was a child prodigy pianist. She performed as a soloist for the *Chicago Symphony* at 17. I grew up in a musical environment, and my focus was on piano. Still, like many boys, I was fascinated by the drums. When I was 10, my mother found a drum teacher, and for almost a year, I used my two drumsticks and practice pad to learn all the rudiments of drumming. These exercises helped me immensely with timing and hand technique, which proved invaluable for my piano playing. Still, unfortunately, my teacher was strict and one-dimensional. I was never allowed to play on a drum set, so I lost interest in playing the drums.

Tad Sisler's Mother, Elaine Witt Sisler at age 16
Source – Sisler Private Collection

However, I stayed with music, and I've had a fantastic career as a performer, producer, composer, editor, and author. On stage as a musician and band leader, I've enjoyed working thousands of gigs and recording sessions with the best drummers on the planet. As an author, I recently won a coveted **Reader's Favorite Award** for a biography I wrote on the life of a famous trumpeter. As a pianist and keyboardist, I learned the nuances of performing using both hands on multiple keyboards and both feet on pedals while singing. I understand how hard it is to play the drums proficiently. Most of the challenge is just getting through the learning experience through hours of practice and coordination exercises. If you want it bad enough, like I did, you can have an extremely rewarding experience for years.

Playing drums is a lot of things, but two things always stood out to me as I watched the greatest drummers perform.

The first was their hand-to-eye coordination and the ability to synchronize their hands and feet to play complicated polyrhythms effortlessly. The second and vastly more important thing was timing.

There's a saying I've heard, **"*So many drummers, so little time!*"** Yes, I've heard groupies say that, but mainly, musicians who perform with so many drummers who begin to rush, or their timing is all over the place as a song or a night of performing progresses.

Locking in your timing is more valuable than any significant ability to play complicated rhythms. The other important considerations for a first-call drummer are playing in the pocket and not overplaying unless the gig calls for it. Music has always been in my blood. This fact made it easier for me to learn because I had a burning desire to improve every day. If you have that burning desire, you will cruise through any setbacks or difficulties and shine.

My friend **Andy Fraga, Sr.** was a great piano player, performing with many iconic artists while he was alive. When my twins were in the 7th grade choir, **Andy's** son, **Andrew Fraga, Jr.** was in the 8th grade band. He sat behind my twins in a performance, banging a cymbal when it was his turn. As time passed, I watched Andrew become a proficient teenage drummer, doing paid gigs at 14. When Andy Sr.'s heart began to fail, I promised him I'd keep an eye on his kid, and after he died, I kept my promise, making Andrew my business partner. We worked as music developers for Yamaha Corporation of America for ten years. He went on to play first as a lead percussionist for major Broadway Shows and then as a first-call drummer for almost every major headliner in existence. Today, he is known as one of the world's finest drummers. His persistence and dedication to the craft made him into what he is today, a far cry from that cymbal-crashing thirteen-year-old I first saw perform.

Andrew Fraga, Jr.
Credit – Fraga Personal Collection

Stick with it and enjoy the process. I promise it will be worth it!

INTRODUCTION

A staggering fact reveals that approximately 90% of people who start learning a musical instrument quit within the first year, often due to frustration with slow progress, lack of time, or insufficient guidance. This high dropout rate underscores the challenges faced by beginners. This is why effective practice methods, motivation, and support systems help you sustain long-term commitment and success learning how to play drums.

When learning any instrument, everyone struggles in the beginning. Immediately, doubts creep in, such as:

How am I going to balance practice with other responsibilities?
What if I feel stuck and I'm not improving quickly?
What happens when I deal with hand, wrist, or foot fatigue?
How can I work all the drum equipment?
How will I stay motivated?

SELF-DISCIPLINE

Many people have told me, *"I always wanted to learn how to play drums, but I have no self-discipline."* Self-discipline is not something you have or don't have. It's something you make happen.

Whether you're a religious person or not, you can understand the concept that when God created us, we were given this amazing power to choose, a power so strong that we actually can use it to choose against God if we want to. I understand the power of addictions, but we can choose to overcome smoking or drugs, or anything we put our minds to. Self-discipline is your choice. You can become the best at what you do if you decide that there is no other option but success. This all starts with self-discipline, with your choice to make it happen, and then to persist until you've succeeded. It's that simple. If you don't believe you can learn an instrument, you probably won't. But, I promise you, if you follow the wisdom and resources of this book, you will find your way if you stick with it.

If you understand from the start that you are not alone and that virtually everyone starts at the same point that you did, it will help you focus on how you will feel when you master the drums. In this book, I focus on the following benefits:

Mastering Basic and Advanced Techniques: Mastering basic and advanced drumming techniques for better performance and ability

Reading Music: Understanding drum notation to play a broader range of music enhances your experience and ability to collaborate.

Playing with Others: Gaining the skills to play in a band or ensemble.

Playing a Variety of Genres and Styles: Learning to adapt to different musical settings and demands.

Improving Timing and Rhythm Precision: Knowing how to keep steady beats and sync with other musicians.

Personal Satisfaction Through Confidence: Building confidence through structured learning and regular practice leads to a more enjoyable drumming experience.

Professional Development: Developing skills to pursue a career or advanced studies in music. Knowing the 'inside scoop' and learning nuances from the masters.

This book is designed to guide you through your drumming journey. It highlights the importance of mastering techniques, understanding rhythms, and, most importantly, enjoying the process.

I will give you a step-by-step approach suitable for all skill levels. Through the book, I will do my best to motivate and encourage you with my knowledge, ideas, and the words of the great masters who came before you.

My friend, **Marty Morell**, is a famous jazz drummer who played with jazz legend **Bill Evans** for seven years.

I had the pleasure of producing a fantastic project called *Jazz Masters: The Barcelona Sessions* with **Marty**, with originals by **Marty**, me, and others, and an ensemble of the best jazz players on the planet. Even though he was at the pinnacle of success, he still solicited feedback from everyone, including **Bill Evans,** in his early career. When asked if **Evans** had critical feedback after his first gig, **Marty** responded:

"He said everything was perfect. Bill let you find your way. He did tell me months later, 'You may want to add a third cymbal to offset behind the bass.' So, I did. I added a bigger one, what's called a China splash cymbal. It has a sizzling sound."

Marty was fearless in accepting advice or criticism. This quality is the mark of the professional. **Marty** also became a master, and he was the most skilled and efficient drummer I've ever witnessed. Always be open to feedback as you go through this journey. Believe in yourself, go with the flow, and you, too, can become a master.

Tad Sisler in his Studio with Marty Morell
Source – Sisler Private Collection

A BRIEF HISTORY OF DRUMS

Drumming is one of the oldest forms of musical expression, dating back thousands of years to early human civilizations. The earliest drums were probably created by our ancestors stretching animal skins over hollowed-out logs or other resonant objects. Early man used drums for communication, rituals, and religious ceremonies to bring communities together. In ancient Egypt, Mesopotamia, and China, drums played significant roles in cultural and religious practices, often accompanied by other percussive instruments. As human societies developed, so did the complexity and variety of drums.

By the Middle Ages, drums had evolved into more structured instruments like the tabor, usually played with a pipe in European military and ceremonial settings. Drums continued to evolve through the Renaissance and Baroque periods, with the development of the snare drum and timpani. Percussion instruments evolved through the ages in different cultures all over the world.

The modern drum set took shape in the early 20th century, driven by the rise of jazz music in the United States. Innovators like **William F. Ludwig** helped develop the bass drum pedal, allowing drummers to play multiple drums simultaneously. This innovation led to the creation of the drum kit, which typically includes a bass drum, snare drum, toms, hi-hat, and various cymbals.

DRUMMING AROUND THE WORLD

Drumming styles and techniques vary widely across cultures, each with unique rhythms and instruments. In West Africa, drumming with the djembe is an enormous part of cultural expression. Djembes are played with bare hands, producing a wide range of tones and rhythms, often accompanied by other drums like the dundun. In Latin America, Afro-Cuban drumming traditions produced the conga and bongo drums, a great part of genres like salsa and rumba. These drums are played with open hands and produce distinct rhythmic patterns. In Asia, drumming traditions are equally diverse. In Japan, the taiko drum is used in both religious ceremonies and energetic performances, usually involving groups of drummers. Indian classical music features the tabla, a pair of drums that require intricate finger and palm techniques. In the Middle East, the darbuka, the goblet drum, is popular in traditional and contemporary music, producing sharp, staccato sounds. Each drumming style reflects the cultural and historical contexts from which they emerged, showing how universally important rhythm has become in human expression. Modern drumming draws on these global traditions, incorporating elements from various drumming cultures into contemporary music.

CHAPTER ONE
GETTING STARTED WITH DRUMMING

ARTIST SPOTLIGHT
RINGO STARR

Ringo Starr
Credit – Wikimedia Commons

T housands of great drummers have come and gone. Still, no single drummer impacted his genre more than **Ringo Starr**, the iconic drummer from **The Beatles** who went on to solo stardom.

Ringo Starr, born **Richard Starkey** in Liverpool, England, on July 7, 1940, faced many challenges from a young age. Growing up in the Dingle district, **Ringo** experienced health struggles in his early years, including a severe case of peritonitis at age six, which left him bedridden for months. Later, he contracted tuberculosis, which kept him in a sanatorium for two years. While he was confined, he discovered his love for drumming. The hospital staff encouraged patients to join the hospital band, and **Richard** found solace and passion in the rhythmic beats of the drums.

Richard's education suffered, and he had trouble finding a job when returning to everyday life. Despite these setbacks, he immersed himself in the local skiffle and rock 'n' roll scenes. He joined the **Eddie Clayton Skiffle Group**, where he started to gain recognition for his drumming. His talent really began to shine when he joined **Rory Storm and the Hurricanes**, one of Liverpool's top bands. At this point, he changed his "stage name" to **Ringo.** Despite the band's local success, **Ringo** struggled with self-doubt and the uncertainty of a stable future in music. Financial instability and the pressure to find a "real job" loomed large, but his love for drumming kept him going.
In fact, his father would tell him constantly that he was wasting his time and that he should just go and work at the local factory.

In 1962, **Ringo's** life transformed when **John Lennon** and **Paul McCartney** asked him to join **The Beatles**, replacing **Pete Best**.
Some fans and even the band's manager, **Brian Epstein**, initially resisted it. The other three members of **The Beatles** saw **Ringo's** unique charisma and solid drumming style **in** the group. His steady beats and distinctive fills quickly became the backbone of **The Beatles'** sound, but fame brought its own challenges. The relentless touring schedule, the pressure to constantly produce hit records, and the invasive media attention were intense. At times **Ringo** struggled with the demands of fame, often feeling overshadowed by his more prominent bandmates.

Despite these struggles, **Ringo's** contributions to **The Beatles** were invaluable. His inventive drumming on tracks like *"Come Together,"* *"Rain,"* and *"A Day in the Life"* showcased his ability to enhance a song's feel and dynamics. **Ringo's** style was not about technical prowess but about serving the music. This philosophy earned him respect among musicians and fans alike. I personally learned from **Ringo** that great drummers think outside the box.

Ringo was one of the first to discard conventional thought and create beats that brought many songs to a new level. *"Come Together"* is a great example of a song that may not have been so hip if **Ringo** had not created its unique drum part.

After **The Beatles** disbanded in 1970, **Ringo** faced the daunting task of establishing a solo career. Overcoming personal and professional obstacles, he released successful albums. He continued to perform, earning his place as a beloved figure in rock history. His journey from a sickly child in Liverpool to a global drumming icon is a great example of resilience, creativity, and enduring passion for music. Never give up! Believe in yourself and stay the course.

"I never studied anything, really. I didn't study the drums. I joined bands and made all the mistakes onstage." – Ringo Starr

Our goal is to help you avoid the embarrassment of making mistakes onstage and become as innovative as **Ringo**!

FEMALE DRUMMERS

During the last century, males dominated the drumming profession in many ways, but many excellent female drummers have significantly impacted the craft. I strongly encourage females to follow their passion in everything they do. If you are a female choosing to play drums, you may gain confidence by studying the work of these legendary trailblazing female drummers:

Sheila E.: The *"Queen of Percussion,"* **Sheila E.** has worked with legendary artists like **Prince, Ringo Starr**, and **Beyoncé.** She's a trailblazer in the industry because of incredible talent on the drums and percussion combined with charismatic stage presence.

Cindy Blackman Santana, married to **Carlos Santana,** is a powerhouse jazz and rock drummer. She's best known for her work with **Lenny Kravitz** and dynamic solo performances. **Cindy's** technical proficiency and ability to blend jazz improvisation with rock energy have earned her a place among the drumming elite.

Meg White: As the drummer for **The White Stripes, Meg White** brought a minimalist and raw approach to drumming that became a defining characteristic of the band's sound. Her simple yet effective style has influenced many musicians and contributed to the resurgence of garage rock in the early 2000s.

Anika Nilles is a German drummer known for her intricate grooves, technical skill, and modern approach to drumming. Her *YouTube* videos have generated millions of views. **Anika** is a very a popular figure in the drumming community.

Anika's ability to blend odd-time signatures with groove-oriented playing has set her apart as a contemporary drumming virtuoso.

Terri Lyne Carrington is a *Grammy-winning* jazz drummer, composer, and producer. She has played with jazz greats like **Herbie Hancock** and **Wayne Shorter. Terri's** versatility and creativity in drumming and composition have made her a highly respected figure in jazz and beyond.

I was blessed to hire and work with **Terri Lyne Carrington** as a featured percussionist on my first big album, *"So Good to Come Home To."* So Good *was* played on American radio in over 100 US cities and sold extremely well.

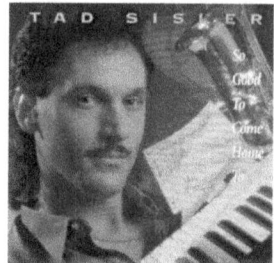

Source – Sisler Private Collection

SECTION ONE
CHOOSING YOUR DRUM KIT

Acoustic Drum Kits are the traditional choice for many drummers. They are known for their rich, organic sound and dynamic range. These kits typically consist of a bass drum, snare drum, tom-toms, hi-hat, and various cymbals (crash, ride, and sometimes splash or china cymbals). Acoustic drums consist of wood shells and metal hardware, with drumheads that can be tuned to achieve different pitches and tones. The sound produced by an acoustic drum kit results from the drummer's technique, the drumheads, the drum shells, and the room's acoustics. Acoustic kits are favoured for live performances and recording in rock, jazz, blues, and classical music, due to their natural resonance and the ability to produce subtle nuances in playing dynamics.

Electronic Drum Kits, or e-kits, offer a modern alternative to traditional acoustic drums. These kits use rubber or mesh pads that trigger electronic sounds when struck. The pads are connected to a drum module (or brain) that produces a wide array of sounds, from realistic acoustic drum samples to synthesized tones. Electronic drum kits are highly versatile and allow drummers to practice quietly with headphones, making them ideal for home practice and environments where noise is a concern. They also offer features like recording capabilities with built-in metronomes and connecting to computers or other electronic devices for music production. Electronic kits are popular in electronic music, pop, and hip-hop, where precise control over drum sounds and integration with digital audio workstations (DAWs) is beneficial.

When I was a young performer in the 1980s, the very hippest drummers used the very first electronic kit, the *Simmons SDS-V*. It looked futuristic with distinctive hexagonal drum pads, and you hear this signature sound on many recordings from that era, including *"Against All Odds"* by **Phil Collins**. Modern electronic drums are far more sophisticated.

Hybrid Drum Kits combine elements of both acoustic and electronic kits, providing the best of both worlds. These kits typically feature standard acoustic drums augmented with electronic drum pads and triggers. The triggers can be attached to acoustic drumheads to capture the drummer's playing and send the signals to a drum module, allowing for electronic sound manipulation. This setup enables drummers to switch seamlessly between acoustic and electronic sounds or blend them for a unique sonic palette. Hybrid kits are particularly useful in live performances where diverse sounds are needed without switching between different kits. They are also advantageous in studio settings, offering a vast range of sounds and the ability to record acoustic and electronic elements simultaneously. From the old Roland M4 units, I've been using triggers on my drum sets in our studios for years. It's cool because you have the midi file of the performance along with the original drums, so you can switch out a sound if you're not happy with it, if you have great separation in your drum mics on the original recording. Due to their flexibility and creative potential, hybrid kits are gaining popularity across various genres, including rock, pop, and experimental music.

"When you approach this instrument for the first time, what comes out of you is simply what you feel." – Dennis Chambers

Dennis Chambers
Credit – Wikimedia Commons

HOW TO SET UP A DRUM KIT

Here's a step-by-step guide to help you set up your drum kit efficiently for comfort, playability, and ergonomics:

CHOOSE THE RIGHT LOCATION: Ensure you place the drum kit on a flat, stable surface. Make sure there's enough space for the entire kit and for you to move comfortably.

ASSEMBLE DRUM STANDS AND HARDWARE: Attach the bass drum pedal to the hoop of the bass drum. Assemble the hi-hat stand and place it to your left (for right-handed drummers). Set up the snare stand in front of where you will sit. Assemble the cymbal stands and place them around the kit where they are easily reachable.

POSITION BASS DRUM: Place the bass drum centrally, facing forward. Extend the bass drum spurs (legs) to prevent the drum from moving.

MOUNT TOMS: If you mount your toms on the bass drum, attach them securely using the mounting hardware. Position the toms at a comfortable height and angle for easy reach and playability.
The floor tom should be placed to the right of the bass drum (for right-handed drummers), adjusting the height to be level with the mounted toms.

BEST DRUM KITS

Choosing the best drum kit depends on your skill level, musical style, and budget.

As you progress as a drummer, you will find that you like certain sets or brands over others. Most pro drummers I work with have several sets for different applications. They may bring a jazz kit to a jazz gig or a kit with a larger kick and more biting snare drum to a gig with a bigger audience, for instance. I've seen drummers substitute their favorite snare from another set. It's entirely up to what you think sounds the best.

HARDWARE MAINTENANCE

Maintaining your hardware is like doing preventative maintenance on your car. It will directly impact your performance quality and equipment longevity. Neglecting maintenance can lead to mechanical failures, inconsistent sound, and even possibly injuries due to malfunctioning hardware. Prioritize maintenance so you can focus on your playing without worrying about technical issues interrupting your flow.

Start by lubricating pedals and stands. Over time, the moving parts of pedals—such as hinges, springs, and chains—and the joints of stands can accumulate dust and become stiff or corroded. This stiffness can impede the fluid motion required for precise footwork and quick adjustments. Appropriate lubricants reduce friction between moving parts, ensuring smooth operation and responsiveness.

Well-lubricated pedals enhance speed and control for bass drum and hi-hat techniques, while smoothly operating stands allow for effortless positioning of drums and cymbals, contributing to a stable and ergonomic setup.

Replacing worn-out parts and accessories is equally important to maintain the functionality and safety of the drum kit. Components like drumheads, cymbal felts, tension rods, and snare wires experience wear and tear through regular use. Worn drumheads can lead to poor tone and reduced responsiveness, while damaged tension rods may cause tuning instability. Inspect parts regularly and replace them when necessary to prevent unexpected failures that could disrupt a performance or practice session.

"Playing fast around the drums is one thing. But to play music, to play with people for others to listen to, that's something else. That's a whole other world." — Tony Williams

Tony Williams
Credit — Wikimedia Commons

PEARL ROADSHOW DRUM SET: **Best For:** Beginners
•9-ply poplar shells
•Complete package with cymbals, hardware, and throne
•Affordable price point
Pros: Great starter kit with everything included, good sound quality for the price
Cons: Cymbals may need upgrading as skills improve

YAMAHA STAGE CUSTOM BIRCH
Best For: Intermediate to Advanced
•100% birch shells for a bright, punchy sound
•High-quality hardware
•Versatile configuration options
Pros: Excellent build quality, outstanding tonal range, ideal for live and studio use
Cons: Cymbals and additional hardware sold separately.
If you have the budget for a better set, **Yamaha Recording Series** drums may be the best professional drums on the market.

DW PERFORMANCE SERIES: **Best For:** Professionals
•North American maple shells
•HVX shell technology for superior resonance
•Customizable finishes and configurations
Pros: Professional-grade sound, durable construction, wide tonal range
Cons: High price point, not suitable for beginners

TAMA IMPERIALSTAR:
Best For: Budget-Friendly Option
•Poplar shells for warm, full sound
•Includes Meinl HCS cymbals and hardware
•Sturdy double-braced hardware
Pros: Great value for money, complete package, reliable and durable
Cons: Cymbals are entry-level, limited finish options

GRETSCH CATALINA MAPLE:
Best For: Jazz and Fusion Drummers
•7-ply maple shells for warm, rich tones
•30-degree bearing edges for enhanced response
•Vintage-style hardware
Pros: Warm, versatile sound, classic look, great for jazz and fusion
Cons: No cymbals included; hardware may need upgrading

ROLAND TD-27KV V-DRUMS:
Best For: Electronic Drumming
•High-resolution, responsive mesh heads
•Advanced digital triggering technology
•Customizable sounds and connectivity options
Pros: Quiet practice, extensive sound library, durable and responsive pads
Cons: Expensive, requires external amplification for live performance and feel for your playing style.

LUDWIG BREAKBEATS BY QUESTLOVE:
Best For: Compact and Portable Setup
•Compact 4-piece configuration
•7-ply hardwood shells
•Designed in collaboration with **Questlove**
Pros: Highly portable, great for small spaces and gigs, stylish design
Cons: Smaller size may limit volume and projection; no cymbals included

CHOOSING THE RIGHT SNARE
Drummers use different snares for different purposes. There are many types of snare drums, each varying in size and material, suited to various musical styles. Here's an overview of common snare drum types:

Standard 14" Snare Drum
Size: 14" diameter, 5.5" to 6.5" depth.
Best for: Rock, pop, jazz, and concert settings.
This is the most common size for a snare drum, offering a balanced mix of depth, tone, and versatility. It provides a full, resonant sound that works well in many styles of music.

Piccolo Snare Drum
Size: 13" to 14" diameter, 3" to 4" depth.
Best for: Funk, hip-hop, and Latin music.
The Piccolo snare produces a high-pitched, crisp sound with minimal depth. Its tight, bright tone makes it great for cutting through mixes, particularly in genres that rely on sharp accents and syncopation.

Deep Snare Drum
Size: 14" diameter, 6.5" to 8" depth.
Best for: Rock, metal, and heavier genres.
With its deeper shell, this snare produces a low, powerful sound with more resonance and body, making it ideal for loud, aggressive genres where the snare needs presence.

Soprano Snare Drum
Size: 12" to 13" diameter, 5" depth.
Best for: Experimental, jazz, and lighter rock.
Soprano snare drums have a higher pitch than standard snares and are often used as secondary drums to add variety to the drum sound. Their brighter, more cutting tones can complement the main snare sounds.

Marching Snare Drum
Size: 14" diameter, 12" depth.
Best for: Marching bands, drum corps.
Known for their deep, articulate tone, marching snares have a high tension and are designed to project across long distances. They produce a sharp, loud sound with tight articulation, which is ideal for precision in outdoor settings.

Wooden Snare Drum
Material: Maple, birch, or mahogany wood shells.
Best for: Jazz, folk, and acoustic settings.
Description: Wooden snare drums produce a warmer, more resonant tone. They are often favored in more nuanced and dynamic genres where the snare sound needs to blend with the overall music without being overly sharp.

Metal Snare Drum
Material: Steel, brass, or aluminum shells.

Best for: Rock, metal, punk.

Metal snare drums have a bright, cutting tone. They have more attack and projection than wooden snares, making them ideal for genres where the snare needs to be loud and aggressive.

SNARE WIRES

The **snare wires**, or **snares**, are a set of metal wires stretched across the bottom resonant head of the snare drum. When the top drumhead is struck, the snares vibrate, producing the distinctive "buzzing" or "rattling" sound.

WHEN TO USE SNARE WIRES

With Snare Wires Engaged: The snare wires are typically engaged for most styles of music, as they provide the sharp, staccato sound that defines the snare drum. This is crucial for genres like **rock, pop, funk**, and **jazz**, where a crisp backbeat is important.

Without Snare Wires (Snare-Off Playing): When the snares are disengaged, the drum produces a sound closer to a tom, with more resonance and less "crack." This is sometimes used in **marching band music, Latin genres**, or **experimental settings** where a more open, resonant drum sound is desired.

By controlling the tension of the snare wires (using the strainer on the side of the drum), drummers can adjust the drum's sensitivity and tone.

Tightening the wires creates a sharper, more defined sound while loosening them creates a softer, looser buzz.

TYPES OF TOMS FOR PRO DRUM SETS

Just as snares are sometimes interchanged, a drummer may add a floor tom, for instance, in a larger band setting for more intensity. Here are common types of tom-toms:

Rack Toms (Mounted Toms)

Sizes: Typically range from **8" to 13"** in diameter, with a depth of **7" to 10"**.
Best for: Rock, pop, jazz, funk, metal.

Rack toms are mounted on the bass drum or on separate stands and are known for their high-pitched, punchy sound. These toms are frequently used for fast fills and accents. Smaller rack toms (8" or 10") are common in jazz and funk for tighter, more controlled tones, while larger toms (12" or 13") are favored in rock and metal for a fuller, more resonant sound.

Floor Toms

Sizes: Generally **14" to 18"** in diameter, with a depth of **12" to 16"**.
Best for: Rock, metal, jazz, fusion, blues.

Floor toms are usually positioned on the floor with legs and offer a deeper, more resonant tone. Due to their powerful low-end thump, the 14" and 16" floor toms are popular in many styles, particularly rock and metal.

Jazz drummers may favor smaller floor toms (like 14") for a more controlled sound, while in heavy metal, an 18" floor tom is often used to add significant depth and power to drum fills.

Concert Toms (Single-Headed Toms)
Sizes: Vary, typically from **8" to 16"** in diameter.
Best for: Orchestral music, concert bands, fusion, and some classic rock.
Concert toms are single-headed drums, meaning they only have a top head (no resonant head). They produce a short, punchy sound with a more defined attack and less sustain. Due to their quick, cutting tone, these toms were popular in classic rock and fusion in the 1970s and '80s.

Power Toms
Sizes: Typically deeper than standard rack toms, with diameters from **10" to 16"** and depths of **10" to 12"**.
Best for: Rock, metal.
Power toms are designed with extra depth to produce a fuller, more resonant sound.
The extended depth enhances the low-end frequencies, making these toms ideal for loud, aggressive music like hard rock and metal.

Fusion Toms
Sizes: Commonly **10", 12", and 14"** in diameter.
Best for: Fusion, funk, jazz, pop.
Fusion tom setups typically consist of smaller toms (10", 12", 14") that are tightly tuned to produce a more defined, higher-pitched sound. These sizes are perfect for genres emphasizing quick, intricate fills and precision, like funk and fusion.

Floor Tom Conversion
Sizes: Usually **14" or 16"** floor toms converted into bass drums.
Best for: Jazz, acoustic, and experimental setups.
In smaller acoustic or jazz setups, drummers may convert floor toms into bass drums for a compact and mellow kit. This setup provides versatility for jazz and experimental genres where a subtler, quieter bass drum sound is needed.

HOW TO CHOOSE DRUMSTICKS
Here are vital considerations to help you select the best drumsticks for comfort, technique, and overall sound:

MATERIAL: Wood is the most common material that offers a natural feel and warm sound.
•**Hickory:** The most popular choice for balancing strength, flexibility, and shock absorption.

•**Oak:** Heavier and more durable, providing a solid feel and higher durability.
•**Maple:** Lighter and more flexible, ideal for fast playing and intricate patterns.
•**Synthetic:** Made from carbon fiber or plastic, offering more excellent durability and consistency.
Pros: Long-lasting, resistant to weather changes, and consistent weight and balance.
Cons: Can lack the natural feel and sound of wood.

SIZE AND WEIGHT
Diameter: Measured in inches, typically ranging from 7A (thinner) to 2B (thicker).
•**Thinner Sticks (e.g., 7A):** Lighter and easier to handle, suitable for jazz, light playing, and beginners.
•**Thicker Sticks (e.g., 5A, 5B, 2B):** Heavier and more durable, providing more power and volume, suitable for rock, metal, and heavier genres.
Length: Typically ranges from 15 to 17 inches.
•**Shorter Sticks:** Provide more control and precision, ideal for fast playing and intricate patterns.
•**Longer Sticks:** Offer greater reach and leverage for powerful, dynamic playing.

TIP SHAPE AND MATERIAL
Tip Shape: Affects the sound and articulation.
•**Round Tip:** Produces a bright, focused sound, ideal for cymbal work and jazz.
•**Oval Tip:** Offers a balanced sound, suitable for various styles.
•**Tear Drop Tip:** Provides a warm, rich tone, great for rock and pop.
•**Barrel Tip:** Produces a punchy, loud sound, suitable for heavy genres like metal.
Tip Material:
•**Wood Tips:** Provide a natural, warm sound but can wear down quickly, especially on cymbals.
•**Nylon Tips:** More durable and consistent, offering a brighter sound, especially on cymbals.

TAPER
Short Taper: Provides more power and durability, suitable for heavy playing.
Long Taper: Offers more flexibility and faster rebound, ideal for quick, intricate playing.

GRIP AND COATING
Natural Finish: Offers a traditional feel with no added grip.
Lacquered Finish: Provides a smooth, glossy finish, which can be slippery when hands get sweaty.

Grip Coating: Features rubberized or textured coatings for better grip, which helps maintain control during extended playing sessions.

"It's been years and years and years I've been playing the drums, and they're still a challenge. I still enjoy using drumsticks and a snare drum." – *Charlie Watts*

Charlie Watts
Credit – Wikimedia Commons

SPECIALTY STICKS

Brushes: These are made from metal or plastic bristles and are used for softer, swishing sounds in jazz and acoustic settings.

Rods/Blasticks: Bundles of thin dowels provide a sound between sticks and brushes, ideal for acoustic and low-volume playing. The first time I heard my drummer. **Steve Neilen,** play with rods, it blew me away. We were on a corporate gig, so we had to be aware of the volume, but brushes weren't cutting it for the song. Rods were the perfect compromise.

Mallets: Feature soft, padded heads used for cymbal rolls and timpani-like effects on drums.

TIPS FOR CHOOSING DRUMSTICKS

Try different sticks in a music store to see how they feel and sound. Match the sticks to your style and the genres you often play. Ensure the sticks feel comfortable in your hands and provide reasonable control and balance. Consider the durability of the sticks, especially if you play heavy genres or perform frequently.

BEST CYMBALS AND BRANDS

Selecting the best cymbals involves considering your musical style, sound preferences, and budget. Leading brands like **Zildjian, Sabian, Meinl, Paiste**, and **Istanbul Agop** offer high-quality cymbals to suit different needs. You can find the perfect cymbals to enhance your drumming performance by exploring various cymbal types and series.

The better drummers I've worked with had their favorite cymbals. As cymbals are fashioned from different pieces of metal in various ways, even the sound of different cymbals within the same brand and type may sound better than others that appear the same. I've always been a freak about cymbals that sound good and not grating. Even a large crash can sound good or bad, yes?

"The drums have hogged a lot of the credit. We're as much – or more – cymbal players, as we are drummers." – Peter Erskine

Peter Erskine
Credit – Wikimedia Commons

BEST CYMBAL BRANDS

Zildjian: One of the oldest and most respected cymbal manufacturers, known for their wide range of high-quality cymbals.
Popular Series: A Custom, K Custom, S Family, ZBT
Excellent sound quality, durability, and a vast selection of models suitable for all genres and playing styles.

Sabian: Another leading cymbal manufacturer offering a variety of cymbals that cater to different sounds and budgets.
Popular Series: HHX, AAX, B8X, XSR
Known for innovation and a broad range of cymbal sounds, from bright and cutting to dark and complex.

Meinl: Known for their unique and modern cymbal designs, Meinl offers high-quality cymbals for contemporary drummers.
Popular Series: Byzance, Classics Custom, HCS, Pure Alloy
It has a diverse range of sounds and finishes and is popular among rock, metal, and jazz drummers.

Paiste: A Swiss company renowned for their precise manufacturing and consistent quality.

Popular Series: 2002, Signature, PST7, Formula 602
Bright and clear sounds, perfect for genres requiring distinct and articulate cymbal tones.

Istanbul Agop: Known for their handcrafted cymbals, combining traditional methods with modern innovations.
Popular Series: Traditional, Xist, Agop Signature, Mantra
Rich, complex sounds with a unique character, ideal for jazz, fusion, and world music.

BEST CYMBALS FOR DIFFERENT USES

When I say 'best,' I mean 'most popular.' Cymbals are a matter of taste, and professionals tend to lean towards these brands and cymbals:

BEST CRASH CYMBALS

Zildjian A Custom Crash: Bright, crisp sound with quick decay, versatile for various genres.
Sabian HHX Evolution Crash: Warm, explosive sound, suitable for live and studio settings.
Meinl Byzance Traditional Medium Crash: Dark, warm tones with a smooth attack, perfect for jazz and fusion.

BEST RIDE CYMBALS

Zildjian K Custom Medium Ride: Dark, rich sound with excellent stick definition and a warm wash.
Sabian AAX Medium Ride: Bright, clear ping with a cutting bell, ideal for rock and pop.
Paiste 2002 Ride: Bright, glassy tones with a clear bell, perfect for classic rock and metal.

BEST HI-HAT CYMBALS

Zildjian New Beat Hi-Hats: Versatile with a crisp "chick" sound, suitable for various styles.
Sabian HHX Groove Hi-Hats: Warm, articulate sound with an outstanding stick and foot response balance.
Meinl Byzance Jazz Thin Hi-Hats: Smooth, dark tones with a buttery feel, ideal for jazz and acoustic settings.

BEST SPLASH CYMBALS

Zildjian A Series Splash: Fast, bright attack with a quick decay, great for adding accents.
Sabian AAX Splash: Clean, penetrating sound with excellent projection.
Meinl Classics Custom Dark Splash has a dark, complex sound with a quick response, suitable for modern music styles.

BEST CHINA CYMBALS

Zildjian Oriental China Trash: Aggressive, trashy sound with a fast attack, perfect for rock and metal.

Sabian AA Chinese: Bright, explosive sound with a strong attack and short sustain.

Meinl Byzance China: Dark, earthy tones with a quick decay, ideal for jazz and fusion.

KEY CONSIDERATIONS FOR BEGINNERS

Drum kits can vary significantly in price, from affordable starter sets to high-end professional kits. Beginners should initially determine how much they are willing to invest. Entry-level acoustic drum kits are generally cheaper but can still require additional purchases like cymbals, stands, and a drum throne. While sometimes more expensive up front, electronic drum kits often come as complete packages and offer the advantage of silent practice with headphones. Beginners must balance quality and cost, ensuring they invest in a kit that will provide a good learning experience without overspending.

Space is also important when choosing a drum kit. Acoustic drum kits require more room due to their size and the need for proper positioning of each component. They also need space for sound projection, which can be challenging in smaller spaces. On the other hand, electronic drum kits are typically more compact. They adjust easily to fit smaller spaces. They also allow for quiet practice with headphones, making them suitable for apartments or homes where noise might be an issue. Beginners should consider the available space in their homes and choose a kit that fits comfortably without compromising playability.

Portability is an important consideration, especially for drummers who may need to transport their kit for lessons, practice sessions, or performances. Acoustic drum kits are generally more cumbersome and require careful disassembly and reassembly, making them less portable. Electronic drum kits, particularly compact models, are easier to transport and set up. Some electronic kits are designed with foldable frames and detachable components, enhancing their portability. An electronic drum set might be the more practical choice for beginners who anticipate moving their kit frequently. However, an acoustic kit can offer a more traditional drumming experience if portability is less of a concern. Balancing these factors will help beginners select the drum kit that best suits their needs and lifestyle.

TIPS FOR BUYING USED INSTRUMENTS

Many used drums and hardware flood the market. Be careful when purchasing used drums:

Inspecting for Damage When buying used drums and cymbals, you should thoroughly inspect each piece for any signs of damage or wear. Examine the shells for cracks, warping, or other structural issues for drums. Check the bearing edges for smoothness and integrity, as any damage here can affect the drum's tuning and sound quality. Inspect the drumheads for excessive wear, as worn heads must be replaced. For hardware, ensure that the lugs, tension rods, and mounts are in good condition and function properly. When it comes to cymbals, look for cracks, keyholes (damaged mounting holes), or significant dents, which can severely impact their sound and longevity. Minor surface scratches or stick marks are generally acceptable and do not usually affect performance. Unfortunately, if you're buying a used set online on *eBay*, for instance, you'll only have the photos and questions you can ask the seller rather than inspection.

Testing Sound Quality: Sound quality is critical when purchasing used drums and cymbals. If possible, test the drums and cymbals in person before making a purchase. Tune drums up and play them at various dynamic levels to ensure they produce a clear, resonant sound without any unwanted buzzing or rattling. Pay attention to the sustain and tone of each drum. For cymbals, strike them with a drumstick to listen for a consistent, pleasant sound. Ensure there are no dull spots or unpleasant overtones. If you're buying online and can't test the items in person, request audio or video samples from the seller. This lets you understand the sound quality and ensure it meets your expectations.

Negotiating the Price is possible when buying used drums and cymbals. Research the current market value of items you're interested in. Websites, forums, and online marketplaces can provide a good reference point. I always check for similar items on *eBay* or *Craigslist,* and I can get a good assessment of worth. When negotiating, consider the condition of the equipment and any necessary repairs or replacements. Be polite and reasonable when explaining any concerns about the condition or price. Sellers usually negotiate, especially if the items have been listed for a while or if you're buying multiple pieces. Additionally, factor in additional costs such as new drumheads, hardware adjustments, or shipping fees if buying online. You can secure a fair deal on quality used drum gear by being informed and negotiating effectively.

DRUM CASES

Keep your drums pristine by putting them in cases when you are not performing or practicing. Here's a breakdown of different cases with pros and cons to each:

SOFT CASES (Gig Bags) - Soft cases, or gig bags, are made from padded fabric materials such as nylon or polyester.
•Lightweight and easy to carry.

•Often more affordable than hard cases.

•Provide some protection from scratches and minor accidents.

•Limited protection against heavy impacts, drops, or crushing.

•Less durable over time compared to hard cases.

•Not ideal for long-distance travel or shipping.

HARD CASES are typically made from molded plastic, fiberglass, or wood. They provide a rigid shell around the drum for maximum protection.

•Offers superior protection against impacts, drops, and crushing.

•Durable and long-lasting.

•Ideal for touring, long-distance travel, and shipping.

•Heavier and bulkier, making them less convenient for quick or frequent transport.

•Generally more expensive than soft cases.

•Can be cumbersome to store when not in use.

HYBRID CASES combine elements of both soft and hard cases, typically featuring a soft exterior with a semi-rigid or reinforced interior structure.

•Offers a balance of protection and portability.

•Lighter than traditional hard cases but sturdier than soft cases.

•Provides good protection for most gigging and local transport scenarios.

•May not offer as much protection as fully hard cases in extreme conditions.

•Can be more expensive than soft cases without providing the same level of protection as hard cases.

•Limited durability compared to full hard cases over time.

FLIGHT CASES are heavy-duty cases specifically designed for air travel and touring. They are usually constructed with plywood, aluminum, and metal reinforcements.

•Provides the highest level of protection for drums during air travel and shipping.

•Built for extreme conditions, like rough handling and environmental factors.

•Often come with secure locking mechanisms and custom foam interiors.

•Bulky and heavy, making them difficult to carry without wheels.

•The most expensive option among drum cases.

•Overkill for local gigs or casual transport due to size and weight.

"You only get better by playing. If you think you stink, you probably do. I consider every drummer that ever played before me an influence, in every way." – Buddy Rich

Buddy Rich

SECTION TWO
SETTING UP YOUR PRACTICE SPACE

CREATE A COMFORTABLE ENVIRONMENT

Start by choosing the right location for your home. Ideally, this space should avoid high-traffic areas to minimize noise disruption. Invest in ergonomic seating, such as a well-padded, adjustable drum throne, which supports good posture and reduces fatigue during long practice sessions. Ensure your practice area is well-lit to prevent eye strain.

Add adjustable lamps for focused lighting on your sheet music or practice materials. Keep the space free from clutter and choose a quiet area to focus your practice without interruptions.

ESSENTIAL ACCESSORIES

Having the right accessories can significantly enhance your practice sessions. Start with a good pair of drumsticks suited to your playing style and size. Drumsticks come in various materials, weights, and lengths. Just as a professional baseball player chooses his favorite bat, you should choose sticks that feel comfortable in your hands and provide the right balance. A practice pad is cool for silent practice and improving your technique without disturbing others. Metronomes are an excellent tool for you to develop a solid sense of timing and rhythm.

Digital metronomes offer features like different tempo settings, time signatures, and subdivision options. Additionally, consider using a drum mute set or electronic drum kit if noise is a concern, as these can help you practice quietly while still providing a realistic drumming experience.

ORGANIZE A PRACTICE ROUTINE

Start by scheduling regular practice times that fit your daily routine. Consistency is key – even short, daily practice sessions can be more effective than irregular, longer ones.

Set specific, achievable goals for each session, whether mastering a particular rudiment, learning a new song, or improving your speed and precision. Break down larger goals into manageable tasks, helping to keep you motivated and on track. Use a timer to segment your practice into focused intervals, ensuring you cover various aspects of your drumming, such as warm-ups, technique, and repertoire.

KEEP A JOURNAL

Maintaining a practice journal is an excellent way to track your progress and stay motivated. In your journal, record the date, duration of your practice session, and specific exercises or pieces you worked on. Note any challenges you faced, how you addressed them, and any breakthroughs or improvements.

Reflecting on your practice sessions can help identify patterns in your progress and areas that need more attention. Setting short-term and long-term goals in your journal provides a clear roadmap for your drumming journey. Regularly reviewing your journal entries can also be a great source of motivation, reminding you of how far you've come.

ENHANCE PRACTICE WITH TECHNOLOGY

Incorporate technology to make your practice sessions more effective and engaging. Use apps designed for drummers, such as metronome apps, drum machine apps, and recording software. Metronome apps can provide a variety of rhythms and time signatures, while drum machine apps can help you practice playing along with different beats and grooves. Recording your practice sessions allows you to listen back and critique your playing, helping you identify areas for improvement. Numerous online resources, including video tutorials and interactive lessons, can supplement your practice routine and provide new techniques and inspiration.

CREATE A POSITIVE PRACTICE ENVIRONMENT

Decorate your practice space with posters of your favorite drummers or bands and keep a collection of your favorite music nearby for inspiration. Surrounding yourself with elements that remind you of your musical goals can boost your enthusiasm. Ensure that your practice space is comfortable, with a good balance of temperature and ventilation. Taking regular breaks during your practice sessions to stretch and relax can prevent burnout and maintain your physical health. By setting up a well-organized, comfortable, and inspiring practice space, you can create the ideal environment to grow as a drummer and enjoy the process.

"You need to take risks, you never know if the end results will be beautiful or strange, you need to be instantaneous, listening to every moment, without missing a scrap of the music, even if you play a rest." — Brian Blade

Brian Blade
Credit – Wikimedia Commons

SECTION THREE: BASIC DRUM THEORY

Before we discuss the basics of drum theory, let's consider the benefits and techniques of using a practice pad and basic drum tuning. A practice pad allows for quiet practice, improves technique and stick control, builds hand strength, and provides an affordable and portable option for regular practice.

By incorporating various techniques such as basic rudiments, stick control exercises, hand independence drills, dynamic control, tempo training, and warm-up routines, drummers can maximize the benefits of using a practice pad and significantly enhance their overall drumming skills.

PRACTICE PAD BENEFITS
Noise Reduction
•Practice pads are significantly quieter than an acoustic drum set, making them ideal for practicing in noise-sensitive environments.
•Drummers can practice at any time of the day without disturbing neighbors or household members.

Portability
•Practice pads are lightweight and portable, allowing drummers to practice anywhere.
•Ideal for traveling musicians or practicing in different locations like at home, in a park, or backstage before a performance.

Improving Technique and Stick Control
•Practice pads provide a consistent and responsive surface, which helps drummers focus on improving their technique and stick control.
•Useful for working on rudiments, sticking patterns, and developing muscle memory without the distractions of different drum sounds.

Building Hand Strength and Endurance
•Regular practice on a pad helps build hand strength and endurance, as it requires precise control and effort to maintain consistent strokes.

•Drummers can develop stronger and more controlled hand movements, translating to better drum performance.

Affordability
•Practice pads are relatively inexpensive compared to a complete drum set.
•Provides an affordable option for beginners and seasoned drummers to practice regularly without expensive equipment.

PRACTICE PAD TECHNIQUES
•Focus on practicing essential rudiments such as single strokes, double strokes, paradiddles, flams, and drags.
• Use a metronome to keep time and gradually increase speed as accuracy improves.
•Practice exercises from books like "*Stick Control for the Snare Drummer*" by **George Lawrence Stone** to enhance stick control and coordination.
•Concentrate on evenness and consistency in each hand, aiming for identical sound and volume from both sticks.
•Practice patterns that require different movements and rhythms for each hand to develop independence.
• Exercises include alternating single strokes between hands, incorporating accents, and practicing different rhythms with each hand.
•Work on playing at various dynamic levels, from pianissimo (soft) to fortissimo (loud), and practice smooth transitions between dynamics.
•Focus on maintaining control and consistency at each dynamic level, ensuring that both hands produce the same volume and tone.
•Use a metronome to practice keeping steady time and gradually increasing tempo.
• Start slowly to ensure precision, then gradually increase the speed while maintaining accuracy and control.
•Develop warm-up exercises to prepare the hands and wrists for practice and cool-down exercises to prevent strain and injury.
• Include stretching and light drumming exercises to prepare and relax the muscles before and after intensive practice sessions.

TUNING YOUR DRUM KIT
Here are some tips and techniques to help you tune your drums effectively to achieve the best sound and performance:
Start with Fresh Drumheads: Replace old or worn-out drumheads with new ones. Fresh drumheads provide better tone, response, and tuning stability.
Prepare Your Drumhead: Seat the drumhead properly on the drum shell. Place the drumhead on the drum, ensuring it sits evenly around the edge. Press down lightly in the center to seat the head.

Finger-Tighten the Tension Rods: Begin by finger-tightening the tension rods around the drumhead. Turn each tension rod clockwise until they are all snug against the drumhead. This ensures even tension.

Use a Drum Key for Even Tension: Tighten the tension rods with a drum key in a crisscross pattern. Tighten each rod a quarter turn at a time, moving in a star pattern across the drum to ensure even tension. For example, if you start at the top rod, the next one to tighten is the one directly opposite.

Tune Both Heads: Tune both the batter (top) and resonant (bottom) heads. Start with the batter head, then move to the resonant head. Tune both heads to a similar pitch for a balanced or slightly higher/lower tone to achieve different sounds.

Check for Even Tension: Ensure even tension around the drumhead. Press gently with your finger about an inch from each tension rod to check for even tension. Adjust as necessary to eliminate any wrinkles or uneven spots.

Fine-Tune the Drum to achieve your desired pitch and tone. Tap near each tension rod with a drumstick and listen to the pitch. Make minor adjustments until the drumhead is in tune with itself.

Tune to Match Your Kit: Tune each drum to complement the overall sound of your kit. Ensure that the pitch intervals between your drums create a harmonious sound. Common intervals are thirds, fourths, or fifths between toms.

Use Muffling and Dampening: Use muffling techniques to control overtones and sustain. Apply drum gels, rings, or internal mufflers to reduce unwanted overtones. Adjust the amount of dampening to achieve your desired sound.

Tune Drums in a Quiet Environment to accurately hear the pitches. A quiet space allows you to focus on the nuances of the drum's sound without background noise interference.

Tune Regularly: Regularly check and adjust your drum tuning. Drums can go out of tune due to changes in temperature, humidity, and playing dynamics. Regular tuning ensures consistent sound quality.

Experiment with Different Tuning techniques to find your unique sound. Try tuning the batter head higher than the resonant head for a punchy sound or the resonant head higher for more sustain. Explore various tuning combinations to suit different musical styles.

Use Tuning Devices: Consider using a drum tuning device for precision. Drum tuners can help you achieve consistent and accurate tuning by measuring the tension or pitch of the drumhead.

SNARE DRUM TUNING PROCESS

Loosen all the tension rods completely, allowing the drumhead to be seated properly. **Finger-tighten each tension rod until** they are all snug. **Use a drum key to** tighten the rods in a star pattern, making small quarter turns. **Check the pitch near** each tension rod and adjust for even tension.

Tune the resonant head similarly, slightly higher or lower than the batter head, depending on your preference. **Fine-tune by** making minor adjustments to both heads until the drum sounds balanced and pleasing.

Adjusting the Snare Wires: Adjust the tension of the snare wires using the throw-off lever or adjustment knob to balance between a crisp, tight sound and a more open, buzzy tone.

Muffling the Sound: To reduce overtones, use **muffling pads** like **Moongel**, a **removable ring**, or a piece of **damping gel** on the batter head. Some of my friends, in a pinch, also use household items like folded tape or a wallet placed on the drum to achieve a more controlled sound.

Tonal Adjustments: Test the drum by playing and adjusting the tension to achieve a consistent tone across the head. Fine-tune as needed to remove any unwanted overtones or uneven sounds.

"Drumming is not worrying about what you can't do. It's about having fun with what you can do." – Chris Adler

Chris Adler
Credit – Wikimedia Comm

UNDERSTANDING DRUM NOTATION

Drum notation is a way of representing rhythmic patterns and drum parts on paper. Unlike traditional musical notation, which deals with pitch, drum notation focuses on rhythm and the various components of the drum kit.

Each line and space of the staff corresponds to a different drum or cymbal. For example, the snare drum is typically notated on the third space from the bottom, the bass drum on the bottom space, and the hi-hat on the top line. Symbols above or below the staff can indicate techniques like rimshots or accents. Learning to read drum notation allows you to accurately reproduce rhythms, learn new songs, and communicate with other musicians.

READING DRUM NOTATION

To read drum notation, start by familiarizing yourself with the layout of the drum staff. The staff consists of five lines and four spaces, each representing different parts of the drum kit. Drum notation uses standard note heads, stems, and flags to indicate rhythm, just like traditional music notation. However, the placement of these notes on the staff specifies which drum or cymbal to play. Additional symbols provide further detail, such as 'x' for hi-hat and slashes for ride cymbal patterns. Practice reading simple patterns, starting with basic rock beats and gradually incorporating more complex rhythms and fills.

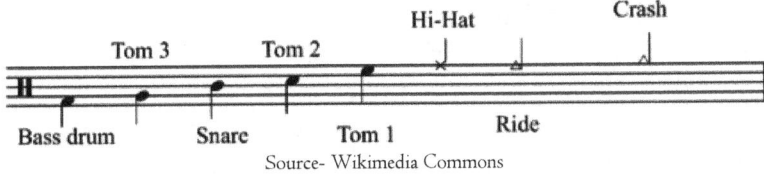

Source- Wikimedia Commons

UNDERSTANDING TIME SIGNATURES

Time signatures in drum notation indicate two things: The top number indicates beats per measure and the bottom number indicates which note value constitutes one beat. The 4/4 time signature is most common, meaning four beats per measure, and the quarter note gets one beat. Other time signatures include 3/4 (three beats per measure) and 6/8 (six beats per measure, eighth note getting one beat). Time signatures help you maintain proper rhythm and flow in a piece of music. Time signatures inform you of the basic pulse of the song and help you align your playing with other musicians. Practice clapping or tapping out different time signatures to internalize the feeling of each.

NOTE VALUES AND RESTS

Note values in drum notation indicate the duration of each hit. Common note values include whole, half, quarter, eighth, and sixteenth notes. Whole notes are held for the entire measure in 4/4 time, half notes for half the measure, and so on. Rests are equally important, indicating periods of silence where no drum or cymbal is played. Each note value has a corresponding rest: whole rest, half rest, quarter rest, etc. Understanding note values and rests allow you to accurately play rhythms and rests, contributing to the overall musicality of a piece. Practice counting and playing different note values to develop a strong sense of timing.

COMBINING NOTES AND RESTS

Combining notes and rests in various patterns creates the rhythms and beats of a piece of music. Drum notation often mixes note values and rests within a single measure to create intricate rhythms. For example, a measure might include a quarter-note bass drum hit, followed by two eighth-note snare hits, and then a half-note rest. Practice reading and playing written drum parts that incorporate a variety of note values and rests, starting with simple patterns and progressing to more complex rhythms.

PRACTICAL APPLICATION

To fully grasp drum notation, apply what you've learned by transcribing and playing along with your favorite songs. Start with simple rock or pop songs that have straightforward drum parts. Write out the notation for the beats and fills, and then practice playing along with the recording. Additionally, consider using drum notation software or apps to help you write and read drum parts more efficiently.

BASIC RHYTHM PATTERNS

The simplest and most used rhythm is the quarter note. In a 4/4 time signature, the most common in Western music, each measure contains four beats, and each quarter note takes up one beat. When drummers play quarter notes, they strike the drum or cymbal on each beat of the measure.

This steady, consistent rhythm is often used in rock and pop music, providing a solid, driving pulse that anchors the song. Quarter notes are also an excellent starting point for beginners to develop a strong sense of timing and rhythm.

Building on quarter notes, eighth notes divide each beat into two equal parts. In a 4/4 measure, this means there are eight eighth notes, each receiving half a beat. Eighth notes are typically notated with a single flag on the stem or connected by a beam between notes. Drummers often use eighth notes to add more energy and complexity to a rhythm. For example, playing eighth notes on the hi-hat while maintaining a quarter-note pulse on the bass drum creates a more intricate and engaging groove. Practicing eighth-note patterns helps you improve timing and develop the ability to play at faster tempos.

Sixteenth notes subdivide the beat, with four sixteenth notes fitting into one beat in 4/4 time. These are notated with two flags on the note stem or two beams connecting the notes. Sixteenth notes add even more complexity and speed to drum patterns, often appearing in fills or more advanced grooves. For example, a drummer might play sixteenth notes on the snare drum to create a rapid, rolling effect or combine sixteenth notes with other note values to craft dynamic, varied rhythms.

Mastering sixteenth notes requires precision and control, as the faster subdivisions demand higher technical skill and coordination.

DYNAMICS

Drumming dynamics refer to the varying levels of volume and intensity with which a drummer plays. Playing softly (piano) and loudly (forte) at appropriate moments can transform a basic beat into something more compelling. For example, a drummer might play the verses of a song with a light touch to create a subtle background rhythm, then switch to a powerful, full-bodied sound for the chorus to emphasize the song's energy and intensity.

Accentuation techniques further expand your dynamic range. Accents involve playing specific notes louder than others within a pattern to create emphasis and add rhythmic interest. For example, accent the backbeat (typically on beats two and four) in a basic rock beat by forcefully hitting the snare drum. This creates a driving pulse that propels the music forward.

Ghost notes, which are very soft, played between the accented beats, add subtle texture and complexity to your playing. Practice single strokes on a practice pad or snare drum, focusing on alternating between soft and loud strokes. Gradually increase the speed while maintaining control over the volume of each stroke. Another helpful exercise is to practice playing paradiddles (a drumming rudiment) while accenting different notes in the pattern.

For example, accent the first note of each four-stroke sequence, then try accenting the second, third, and fourth notes in separate repetitions. These exercises build the muscle memory and coordination needed to execute dynamic variations smoothly and naturally in your playing.

You'll develop greater control incorporating techniques into your daily practice routine over the dynamics of your drumming, allowing you to add depth and expression to your performances.

"There is only one way to learn. It's through action. Everything you need to know you have learned through your journey."
— Paulo Coelho, The Alchemist

Paulo Coelho
Credit – Wikimedia Commons

RECOMMENDED DRUM BOOKS

I strongly suggest books on technique. Instructional books offer valuable lessons, exercises, and insights to help new drummers develop their skills.

I. "Stick Control for the Snare Drummer" by George Lawrence Stone

Often referred to as the "drummer's bible," this book focuses on developing stick control and hand technique through progressive exercises.
•Emphasis on single, double, and triple stroke rolls.
•Exercises to improve speed, control, and coordination.
•Suitable for daily practice routines.
•Provides a strong foundation in drumming fundamentals and is widely recommended by drum teachers.

2. "Progressive Steps to Syncopation for the Modern Drummer" by Ted Reed

A classic book that teaches the principles of syncopation and rhythmic interpretation, essential for all drumming styles.
•Exercises designed to improve rhythmic accuracy and timing.
•Focus on syncopated rhythms and sight-reading.
•Applicable to drum set and snare drum practice.
•Helps drummers understand and play complex rhythms, building a solid rhythmic foundation.

3. "A Fresh Approach to the Drum Set" by Mark Wessels

This book comprehensively introduces the drum set, covering everything from basic techniques to playing complete songs.
•Step-by-step lessons on reading drum notation, basic beats, and fills.
•Includes play-along tracks for practical application.
•Covers different musical styles, including rock, jazz, and Latin.
•Easy-to-follow format with a focus on developing a well-rounded skill set.

4. "Drumming for Beginners" by Scott Schroedl

An accessible guide that covers drumming basics, from setting up the kit to playing various beats and fills.
•Clear explanations and photos for visual learners.
•Lessons on proper hand and foot techniques.
•Introduction to different music genres.
•Provides a straightforward introduction to drumming with practical advice and exercises.

5. "Alfred's Drum Method, Book I" by Dave Black and Sandy Feldstein

A well-structured book that introduces fundamental drumming concepts, focusing on snare drum technique and reading skills.

- Progressive lessons on reading music and developing rudiments.
- Includes exercises and play-along pieces.
- Suitable for individual or classroom instruction.
- Offers a solid introduction to drumming fundamentals, making it a staple in many drum education programs.

6. "The Beginner's Guide to Electronic Drums" by Bob Terry

This book is tailored for those starting with electronic drums, covering everything from setup to advanced playing techniques.
- Instructions on setting up and configuring electronic drum kits.
- Exercises to develop coordination and timing.
- Tips on using electronic drum features and technology.
- Ideal for those who have chosen electronic drums as their starting point, providing specific guidance for this type of kit.

7. "Mastering the Tables of Time" by David Stanoch

A unique approach to understanding rhythm and timing, focusing on the concept of "tables of time" to develop a more profound sense of timing.
- Exercises to improve timing and rhythmic precision.
- Application of concepts to various drumming styles.
- Includes play-along tracks and practice tips.
- Helps drummers develop a solid internal sense of timing and rhythm.

Books with exercises, technique, and theory help accelerate your learning experience. The main thing is to stay focused and progress, even in small amounts. Remember what my friend, Multi-Platinum *Billboard* artist **Rod Stewart** said:

"You've got to have this burning desire in your chest to succeed."

Tad Sisler with Rod Stewart
Source – Sisler Private Collection

CHAPTER TWO
BASIC TECHNIQUES

To learn proper technique, you must incorporate it with timing. The importance of timing for a drummer cannot be overstated. It is the cornerstone of effective drumming, ensuring that the music flows smoothly and that the band stays in sync. Most band leaders I've worked with would rather have a good, solid drummer with impeccable timing power their band over a great drummer with bad timing.

SECTION ONE
TIMING, PROPER GRIP AND STICK CONTROL

THE CRITICAL IMPORTANCE OF TIMING

Timing is the foundation of drumming. It ensures that all band elements are synchronized, creating a cohesive and harmonious sound. Good timing helps maintain the song's structure, allowing other musicians to rely on the drummer to keep the pace steady. A drummer with excellent timing can smoothly transition between different parts of a song, ensuring that tempo changes and rhythmic variations are seamless. This reliability builds trust among band members, making the drummer the backbone of the ensemble. Good timing allows the drummer to lay down a solid rhythm that listeners can move to and that other musicians can lock into. This is especially important in genres like funk, jazz, and hip-hop, where the groove is paramount.

Timing is about playing on the beat and understanding the nuances of playing slightly ahead or behind the beat to create a particular feel.
This sense of timing and groove can transform a simple beat into something alive and engaging, keeping the audience connected to the music.

"Any sound, if it's in time, has some value" – Benny Greb

Benny Greb
Credit – Wikimedia Commons

TECHNIQUES TO IMPROVE TIMING

PRACTICE WITH A MENTRONOME: Using a metronome helps drummers internalize a consistent tempo and trains them to stay on beat. Practice at different tempos with multiple subdivisions (e.g., quarter notes, eighth notes, sixteenth notes) to improve versatility and precision. Start slowly, gradually increasing the speed as your timing improves.

PLAY ALONG WITH RECORDINGS: Choose songs with intense, steady drumming and try to match the timing and feel. Drumless backing tracks are excellent for this purpose as they allow the drummer to fill in the timing role, mimicking a live performance environment.

SUBDIVISION PRACTICE: Practice playing grooves and fills while subdividing the beat into smaller units (e.g., eighth notes, triplets, sixteenth notes). This helps drummers feel the beat more precisely and improves timing accuracy. Incorporate ghost notes and accents to create a more complex rhythmic structure. This not only improves timing but also enhances dynamic control and musicality.

USE A DRUM MACHINE: A drum machine or loop station helps drummers stay on time while allowing them to explore different grooves and rhythmic patterns. Create custom loops at various tempos and practice playing along. This can simulate the experience of playing with a band and improve timing in different musical contexts. I performed poolside at hotels in the Palm Springs, California area for ten years, using a drum machine and a live percussionist. Performing to a drum machine helped me to develop my inner clock, and now I can immediately tell when a drummer is rushing, and forcefully slow them back into the beat if I need to.

RECORD AND ANALYZE YOUR PLAYING: Recording practice sessions and performances allows drummers to listen back and identify timing issues that may not be noticeable while playing. Analyze the recordings to pinpoint specific areas where timing is off. Focus on these areas during practice sessions, using targeted exercises to improve accuracy and consistency.

STICK CONTROL

Proper Grip is fundamental to a drummer's technique, impacting control, speed, and endurance. The most commonly used grip is the matched grip, where both hands hold the drumsticks, similarly, resembling a handshake. There are two main variations of matched grip: **German grip** and **French grip**. In **German grip**, the palms face downward, with the sticks held loosely between the thumb and first two fingers, allowing for powerful strokes. This grip is versatile and often used for rock, pop, and other genres requiring solid and consistent strokes.

On the other hand, **French grip** involves turning the palms to face each other with the thumb on top of the stick. This grip is more relaxed and is favored for fast, intricate playing, such as in jazz or orchestral drumming, as it allows for greater finger control and finesse.

Traditional Grip is another widely used technique, especially in jazz and marching bands. It originated from military drumming when the snare drum was carried at an angle, making playing with one hand in an underhand grip easier. In traditional grip, the left hand (for right-handed drummers) holds the stick between the thumb and first two fingers, with the palm facing upward. The right hand uses a matched grip. This grip is handy for playing ghost notes and intricate patterns, offering a different feel and dynamic range than a matched grip. While traditional grip requires more practice, it remains popular among drummers who appreciate its historical roots and unique control capabilities. Understanding and practicing these different grips allows drummers to choose the most appropriate technique for their playing style and the demands of the music they perform.

STICK CONTROL IMPROVEMENT EXERCISES

Single Stroke Roll: Develops evenness and speed in alternating strokes.
Exercise: •R L R L R L R L
•Start slow, focusing on even volume and timing.
•Gradually increase speed while maintaining control.
•Use a metronome to keep consistent timing.
•Ensure both hands produce an even sound.

Double Stroke Roll: Improves control over double strokes and rebound.
Exercise: •R R L L R R L L
•Begin at a comfortable tempo, focusing on smooth and even strokes.
•Increase speed gradually as control improves.
•Utilize the natural rebound of the sticks.
•Keep a relaxed grip to allow for fluid movement.

Paradiddles: Enhances coordination and control in switching between single and double strokes.
Exercise: •Standard Paradiddle: R L R R L R L L
                •Inverted Paradiddle: L R L L R L R R
                •Paradiddle-diddle: R L R R L L
•Practice at a slow tempo, ensuring clarity and consistency.
•Emphasize the first note of each grouping to develop accents.
•Maintain a steady tempo with a metronome.

Flams: Develops precision and timing in executing flams.
Exercise: •Basic Flam: rL lR

• Flam Tap: rL R lR L
• Flam Accent: rL R L rL R L

• Practice slowly, ensuring the grace note (small note) and primary note (large note) are distinct.
• Focus on maintaining even spacing between the grace note and the primary note.
• Alternate between hands to develop equal control.

Drags: Improves control and timing in executing drags.
Exercise: • Basic Drag: rrL llR
• Drag Tap: rrL R llR L
• Single Dragadiddle: rrL R L R L
• Practice slowly, focusing on the evenness of the drag notes.
• Ensure the drag notes are light and controlled.
• Maintain a relaxed grip to allow for smooth execution.

Finger Control Exercises: Enhances finger dexterity.
• Play single strokes using primarily finger movements.
• Practice alternating finger strokes (e.g., R (fingers) L (fingers)).
• Perform double strokes focusing on finger control.
• Start at a slow tempo to build strength and control.
• Gradually increase speed as finger dexterity improves.

Accent Exercises: Improves control over accented and unaccented strokes.
Exercise: • Accent on Every 4th Note: R l r l R l r l
• Alternating Accents: R L r l R L r l
• Random Accents: Incorporate random accents within a single or double-stroke roll.
• Focus on playing accents louder and unaccented notes softly.
• Maintain a relaxed grip to facilitate quick dynamic changes.
• Use a metronome to keep a steady pulse.

PRACTICE ROUTINE
Begin with 5-10 minutes of basic single and double-stroke rolls at a comfortable tempo. Spend 10-15 minutes on each of the above exercises, focusing on control and precision. End with 5 minutes of slow, relaxed playing to prevent strain and reinforce muscle memory.

AVOIDING COMMON MISTAKES
To avoid common mistakes while practicing, maintain a relaxed grip and proper posture. Tension in the arms and hands leads to fatigue and even injury, so hold the sticks loosely, allowing for natural rebound and minimizing strain. Regularly check for any unnecessary tension by taking short breaks during practice to shake out your hands and relax your muscles. Additionally, pay

attention to stick angles; the sticks should strike the drumheads at a slight angle rather than flat, which helps produce a fuller sound and prevents damage to the drumheads.

SECTION TWO: BASIC RUDIMENTS

Rudiments are the foundational patterns every drummer should master. The **single-stroke roll** is one of the most fundamental rudiments, involving alternating strokes between the left and right hands (R-L-R-L) to create a continuous, even rhythm. This rudiment is essential for developing speed and control. The **double-stroke roll builds** upon the single-stroke roll by requiring each hand to play two consecutive strokes (R-R-L-L). Mastering this rudiment enhances a drummer's ability to play smoother, faster rolls. Another critical rudiment is the **paradiddle**, a versatile four-stroke pattern that alternates between single and double strokes (R-L-R-R, L-R-L-L). Paradiddles can be used to create dynamic fills and grooves, inspiring drummers to experiment with different sounds and textures.

COMBINING RUDIMENTS AND APPLICATION

Once you are comfortable with the basic rudiments, practice combining them to create more complex patterns and rhythms. For example, alternating between single-stroke rolls and double-stroke rolls within the same exercise helps build coordination and fluidity.

Additionally, incorporating paradiddles into more extensive patterns allows you to explore different accents and dynamics. Applying these rudiments to the drum set involves spreading the strokes across different drums and cymbals. For instance, a single-stroke roll can be played between the snare drum and toms, while paradiddles can create intricate hi-hat and snare drum patterns.

PRACTICE ROUTINES/MASTERING RUDIMENTS

A well-rounded practice routine should include dedicated time for each rudiment. Start at a slow tempo to ensure precision and gradually increasing speed as control improves.

You should also practice rudiments with a metronome to continue to develop a strong sense of timing. Incorporating rudiments into daily warm-up exercises helps build muscle memory, while alternating between different rudiments in quick succession enhances coordination and adaptability.

Additionally, creating short drum solos or fills using a combination of rudiments allows you to apply these patterns in a musical context, making practice sessions more engaging and relevant to real-world playing situations. Commit to regular, focused practice.

"Anytime you strike the drums, you have to be aware that you're creating a musical event." — Vinnie Colaiuta

Vinnie Colaiuta
Credit – Wikimedia Commons

USE YOUR PRACTICE PAD TECHNIQUES

As I mentioned earlier, practicing drum rudiments on a practice pad is an excellent way to build control, speed, and precision without the distraction of a full drum kit. Start with the **single stroke roll**, alternating hands (R-L-R-L) at a slow tempo and gradually increasing speed while maintaining evenness and clarity. For the **double stroke roll** (R-R-L-L), focus on getting two clean, distinct strokes from each hand, using wrist motion rather than arm movement. The **paradiddle** (R-L-R-R, L-R-L-L) is another excellent exercise to practice on the pad, allowing you to work on hand independence and accent placement. To enhance these exercises, use a metronome to ensure consistent timing and start with lower tempos to perfect your technique before speeding up.

SECTION THREE
DEVELOPING HAND AND FOOT COORDINATION

BASIC DRUM COORDINATION EXERCISES

One of the foundational coordination exercises involves practicing single hand and foot patterns. For example, start by playing a steady quarter note pulse on the bass drum with your foot while keeping time on the hi-hat with your right hand. Then, add the snare drum on beats two and four with your left hand, creating a basic rock beat. Once comfortable, try alternating hands and feet— play eighth notes on the hi-hat with your right hand while alternating between the bass and snare drums for each beat. This exercise helps build independence between your limbs, allowing you to maintain a steady groove while introducing variations with your hands and feet.

INTRODUCTION TO DRUM FILLS

Drum fills add variety and excitement to your playing by transitioning between different song sections. A simple fill might involve playing a single-stroke roll across the toms, starting with your dominant hand and moving down from the high tom to the floor tom.

Another basic fill is to play four notes on the snare drum, followed by a bass drum hit on the downbeat of the next measure. Integrate them smoothly into your regular beats. Start by playing a basic beat for three measures, then introduce your fill in the fourth measure. Practicing this way helps you develop a sense of timing and ensures that your fills flow naturally within the context of a song.

MASTERING COORDINATION AND FILLS: Slow and deliberate practice helps coordination. Begin slowly to ensure that each note is accurate and that your hands and feet are moving in sync. Use a metronome to keep time, increasing the tempo as you become more comfortable with the patterns. This approach helps build muscle memory and allows you to play more complex rhythms without losing control. But remember, it's not just about the music. Focus on staying relaxed and maintaining proper posture to prevent tension and fatigue. As you gain confidence, experiment with different combinations of hand and foot patterns and create your own fills, applying them in various musical contexts. The best drummers I've used in the studio will use touch sensitivity while playing fills, accenting toms differently to blend emotion and passion into the fill.

CHAPTER THREE
INTERMEDIATE TECHNIQUES
BUILDING REPERTOIRE

ARTIST SPOTLIGHT
DAVE GROHL

Dave Grohl, drummer for **Nirvana** and the frontman of **Foo Fighters,** is a great example of the power of perseverance and passion in overcoming challenges to achieve professional success. **Grohl's** drumming journey began in his teenage years when he taught himself to play by listening to records and mimicking the beats of his favorite bands.

His story reminds us that we all start from the same place with the same challenges, regardless of our field. Without formal training, **Grohl** faced the everyday struggles of many self-taught musicians: mastering the basics, developing proper technique, and building the confidence needed to perform in front of others. Despite these obstacles, **Grohl's** determination and love for music drove him to practice relentlessly, often using pillows as makeshift drum pads to improve his speed and control.

As **Grohl** progressed, he encountered the intermediate challenges that many drummers face, like refining his timing, expanding his rhythmic vocabulary, and integrating more complex patterns into his playing.

During his time with the hardcore punk band **Scream, Grohl** honed his skills by playing live shows and recording albums, pushing himself to experiment with different styles and techniques. When he joined **Nirvana** in 1990, **Grohl** had to adapt to the band's grunge sound, which demanded a balance of power, precision, and subtlety. This period was a significant learning curve, as he worked to perfect his drumming for the band's groundbreaking album, "*Nevermind.*"

Grohl's breakthrough came when his hard work and persistence paid off with the release of "*Nevermind,*" which catapulted **Nirvana** to international fame. His drumming on tracks like "*Smells Like Teen Spirit*" became iconic, showcasing his ability to combine raw energy with tight, controlled playing. This experience solidified **Grohl's** place in rock history and laid the foundation for his future success as a musician and bandleader. It's a testament to the fact that with dedication and a love for the craft, even the most demanding challenges can be overcome on the path to professional success.

Grohl's story inspires me, proving that transformation is possible with relentless drive and a commitment to pushing boundaries and evolving as an artist.

Dave Grohl
Credit – Flickr/Craig – Wikimedia Commons

"I love being a drummer. Everyone thinks you're dumb. What they don't realize is that f it weren't for you, their band would suck."
– Dave Grohl

SECTION ONE
EXPANDING INTERMEDIATE RUDIMENTS
Beyond the basics like single and double stroke rolls, focus on mastering rudiments such as the flam, drag, and double paradiddle. A flam involves playing a soft grace note followed by a louder primary note, adding depth and texture to your playing.

The drag is similar but includes two grace notes before the primary stroke, creating a drag effect. The double paradiddle extends the paradiddle, consisting of six strokes (R-L-R-L-R-R) that offer more rhythmic variation.

APPLYING RUDIMENTS TO THE DRUM KIT

To fully integrate these rudiments into your drumming, practice patience and commitment. Start by applying them across the drum kit. For example, try playing flams on the snare drum while incorporating the bass drum or toms. Drags can be used to embellish fills or accent transitions between beats. The double paradiddle can be spread across different drums, creating intricate, flowing patterns. Practical exercises include playing each rudiment slowly to ensure accuracy and gradually increasing the speed while maintaining control.

Use a metronome to track your progress and focus on developing both speed and precision.

CREATING RUDIMENT COMBOS

To challenge yourself and create unique rhythmic patterns, alternate between flams and double paradiddles or integrate drags into a paradiddle pattern to add complexity. Repeat these combos in various sequences, gradually increasing speed while ensuring each stroke remains precise and controlled to improve your versatility, develop a broader rhythmic vocabulary, and enhance your ability to improvise and create dynamic drum parts.

SECTION TWO
EXPLORING DIFFERENT GENRES

COMMON DRUMMING GENRES

You can have all the chops in the world, but if you don't fit into the genre you are playing, it just won't work. I know many drummers I call 'jazz snobs' because they are fantastic jazz drummers, and they believe that jazz is the only real pure art form a drummer should play.

The best drummers show up for a gig prepared to kick ass to make the band and genre they are playing sound authentic and outstanding, no matter what genre it is.

My friend **Glen Campbell** was a *Billboard Multi-Platinum* singer and guitarist with a string of #1 Hits. Early in his career, he knew the importance of being able to play any genre well.

He became so good that he was a first-call guitarist for hundreds of recording sessions and a member of the famous **"Wrecking Crew"** of studio musicians. **Glen** said:

"I played my country music in clubs around the South till 1961, and then I got lucky and started to pick up session work. I played with some of the biggest in the business...Elvis, Sinatra, Nat 'King' Cole, Sammy Davis, Dean Martin. In one year alone, I played on no less than 586 recording sessions".

Glen Campbell Performing with Tad Sisler
Source – Sisler Private Collection

ROCK
•Heavy backbeat on the 2 and 4 of the measure.
•Powerful and driving rhythms.
•Use of the full drum kit, with a strong emphasis on the bass drum and snare.
•**Basic Rock Beats**: Simple, repetitive patterns that drive the music.
•**Fills**: Often used to transition between song sections.
•**Syncopation**: Adds variety and complexity.
Notable Drummers: John Bonham (Led Zeppelin), Neil Peart (Rush), Dave Grohl (Nirvana, Foo Fighters).

JAZZ
•Swing feel, with a focus on syncopation and improvisation.
•Use of ride cymbal for timekeeping, with lighter snare and bass drum work.
•Complex rhythms and frequent use of polyrhythms.
•**Swing Pattern**: Ride cymbal pattern that emphasizes the triplet feel.
•**Brushes**: Often used on the snare for a softer, smoother sound.
•**Comping**: Complementary rhythms played on the snare and bass drum.
Notable Drummers: Buddy Rich, Max Roach, Art Blakey.

BLUES
•Slow to mid-tempo grooves with a strong shuffle or swing feel.
•Emphasis on groove and feel over technical complexity.
•Frequent use of triplets and dotted rhythms.
•**Shuffle Beat**: A triplet-based rhythm often played on the hi-hat or ride cymbal.
•**Backbeat**: Strong accent on beats 2 and 4, often with a heavy snare.
•**Brushes**: Used for a softer, more laid-back sound.
•**Notable Drummers**: Sam Lay, Fred Below, Steve Jordan.

FUNK

•Highly syncopated rhythms with a strong groove.
•Emphasis on the "one" (the first beat of each measure).
•Use of ghost notes and intricate hi-hat patterns.
•**Groove**: Consistent, repetitive patterns that drive the song.
•**Ghost Notes**: Lightly played notes that add subtle texture and complexity.
•**Syncopation**: Off-beat rhythms that create a funky feel.
Notable Drummers: Clyde Stubblefield (James Brown), David Garibaldi (Tower of Power), Jabo Starks (James Brown).

LATIN

•Intricate rhythms, syncopation, and polyrhythms, often using patterns like the clave.
•Incorporates a wide range of percussion instruments, including congas, timbales, bongos, and cowbells, alongside the drum set.
•Draws heavily from Afro-Cuban and Brazilian musical traditions.
•**Beat:** Syncopated, interlocking patterns emphasizing a danceable, energetic groove.
•**Sticks:** Drumsticks, brushes, or hands, depending upon the desired sound and instrument
•**Beats:** Layered, involving straight and swung rhythms, emphasizing the offbeat, creating a lively, dynamic feel.
•**Notable Drummers:** Tito Puente, Horacio "El Negro" Hernández, Alex Acuña

SECTION THREE
LEARNING AND PLAYING SONGS

SELECTING SONGS TO PRACTICE

Consider your current skill level and the areas you wish to improve. Beginners might start with simple, straightforward beats, while intermediate drummers can challenge themselves with more complex rhythms and fills.

It's important to choose songs that cover a range of genres, as this exposes you to different drumming styles and techniques.

For example, an easy song like *"Billie Jean"* by **Michael Jackson** features a steady, straightforward beat that's perfect for beginners. As you progress, try something more challenging like *"Smells Like Teen Spirit"* by **Nirvana**, which includes a mix of powerful, dynamic drumming and syncopated rhythms. For a different genre, consider practicing *"Superstition"* by **Stevie Wonder**, which incorporates funk grooves that demand precision and feel.

My dear friend **Steve Madaio** was a legendary trumpet player. Together with him, I wrote his biography entitled *"Reflections in the Key of Life."* **Steve** was onstage at **Woodstock** with the **Butterfield Blues Band**, and he spent years recording and touring with **Stevie Wonder.** *"Superstition"* only had three artists on the track. **Stevie Wonder** played drums and all the other instruments on the track, except for the two horns performed by **Steve Madaio** and **Trevor Lawrence.** Stevie was a self-taught drummer although he is known mostly for his outstanding keyboards and vocals, and, of course, for his iconic songwriting. His soulful music transcends all boundaries. **Stevie** said,

"I want to take all the pain that I feel and celebrate and turn it around."

This is the essence of soulful performance. A great player works on emulating this feeling as they practice.

Steve Madaio and Stevie Wonder
Source – Madaio Private Collection

UNDERSTANDING SONG STRUCTURES: Break down the song's structure, identifying key sections such as the verse, chorus, and bridge. The verse typically features a consistent beat that supports the vocals, while the chorus often introduces more energy and variation in the drumming to emphasize the song's hook.

The bridge serves as a transitional section, offering an opportunity to introduce different rhythms or fills. Understanding common song forms, like the AABA or verse-chorus-verse structure, helps you anticipate changes in the music and play more cohesively with the rest of the band. For instance, in *"Back in Black"* by **AC/DC**, the verse and chorus have distinct rhythmic patterns that require you to adjust your playing style to match the dynamics of each section.

As a **Yamaha** developer, I did a lot of drum programming. I noticed that most popular songs start with sparse or no drums and build to a climax in the choruses. When returning to the verse, the drums typically scale back and build again to the next chorus.

PLAYING TO TRACKS AND RECORDING YOUR PERFORMANCES

Playing along with background tracks helps you develop timing, groove, and consistency. Start by choosing tracks with no drums or a clear, steady beat to follow. Focus on staying in time with the music, paying attention to how your drumming complements the other instruments. Recording your practice sessions allows you to listen back and critically assess your performance. Pay attention to timing, dynamics, and how well you maintain the groove throughout the song. For example, practicing along with a drumless version of *"Take Five"* by **Dave Brubeck** can help you work on jazz drumming and improve your ability to navigate unusual time signatures like 5/4. Play to a click whenever you can as a good timing exercise.

CHAPTER FOUR
ADVANCED TECHNIQUES
CREATIVE EXPRESSION

How does the role of improvisation differ between jazz, where it is often the centerpiece of performance, and genres like rock or classical, where improvisation plays a more supporting or unexpected role?

Paul Simon may have said it best:

"Improvisation is too good to be left to chance."

This quote is hilarious to me because the heart of improvisation is chance, and yet, to be good at it, you should think out the fundamentals of what you might play before your performance. I've lived through drum solos that were amazing on every level, and the improvisation was primarily based on the techniques the drummer chose to showcase during the solo. It all ties in together, and you realize that more and more as you grow as a musician.

Paul Simon
Credit – Flickr/David – creativecommons.org
https://www.flickr.com/photos/bootbearwdc/2834526157

SECTION ONE
ADVANCED RUDIMENTS

Let's delve into the world of mastering advanced rudiments and techniques to unlock greater versatility and musical expression. One such versatile rudiment is the **ratamacue**, a compound rudiment that combines a drag (two grace notes) with a triplet figure.

The ratamacue, with its unique, flowing feel, is not just confined to marching band drumming. It can be adapted to various genres, sparking creativity and adding dynamic fills and transitions to your drum patterns.

Another advanced rudiment that equips you for complex rhythms is the **Swiss Army triplet**. This rudiment involves combining a single stroke and a flam to produce a rolling, syncopated effect. It's a practical tool for creating complex, textured rhythms and is commonly employed in snare drum solos and cadences, giving you the edge in your performances.

Inverted paradiddles are another challenging rudiment that flips the traditional paradiddle pattern (R-L-R-R, L-R-L-L) by first starting with the double stroke (R-R-L-R, L-L-R-L). This inversion adds a new level of complexity to the paradiddle, requiring greater control and coordination. Drummers often use inverted paradiddles to create intricate hi-hat and snare drum patterns or to add variation to grooves. To master these advanced rudiments, practice them slowly at first, focusing on precision and evenness, then gradually increase your speed.

COMPLEX STICK CONTROL

Stick control is necessary to push your technique further to enhance your speed, power, and technical ability. **Multiple bounce rolls**, or buzz rolls, involve creating a continuous, sustained roll by allowing the stick to bounce multiple times on the drumhead with each stroke.

This technique requires a delicate balance between grip and stick pressure, producing a smooth, consistent sound. Incorporating multiple bounce rolls into your playing can add a shimmering texture to snare drum parts or be used in drum solos for dramatic effect.

The **Moeller** technique utilizes natural arm motion and rebound to produce powerful yet controlled strokes. It uses a whipping motion to allow you to play with greater speed and dynamics while minimizing fatigue. It's beneficial for playing fast, accented patterns and maintaining endurance during long performances. Combine the **Moeller** technique with advanced stick control exercises, alternating between multiple bounce rolls and single strokes.

POLYRHYTHMS AND CROSS-STICKING

Polyrhythms involve playing two or more different rhythmic patterns simultaneously, often using different limbs. For example, playing a 3-over-2 polyrhythm might involve playing three evenly-spaced notes with one hand while the other plays two evenly-spaced notes simultaneously. Polyrhythms challenge your sense of timing and require a deep understanding of rhythmic subdivision.

Mastering polyrhythms allows you to create intricate, layered rhythms that add complexity and interest to your playing, especially in genres like jazz, progressive rock, and fusion.

Cross-sticking is another advanced technique that involves crossing one stick over the other to play different drums or cymbals without altering your grip or posture. This technique is often used to create interesting rhythmic variations or to add visual flair during performances. To practice cross-sticking, start with simple patterns, crossing from the snare to a tom or cymbal, and gradually incorporate more complex movements.

Combining cross-sticking with polyrhythms can create unique rhythmic textures and improve coordination.

For ten years, I performed poolside in the Palm Springs, California, area at the major resort hotels. I performed with legendary drummer/percussionist Steve **Neilen** for much of that time. **Steve** had impeccable timing and chops; he was one of the strongest drummers who ever backed me up. At poolside, he played percussion and spent an enormous amount of time studying polyrhythms from around the world, including Latin and African rhythms. As a result, he improved daily on his already excellent skills as a percussionist. Study and apply what you learn to your live performances and recordings. Experiment with new ideas always to grow.

Steve Neilen
Source – Sisler Private Collection

SECTION TWO
IMPROVISATION AND SOLOING

Imagine the joy of creating spontaneous drum solos and adding your unique touch to a performance through improvisation. The foundation of improvisation lies in **creating drum solos** by developing a solo "vocabulary"—this involves building a repertoire of rhythmic patterns, fills, and grooves you can draw from during a solo. Start by practicing basic rudiments, such as single-stroke rolls, double-stroke rolls, and paradiddles, and then experiment with combining them in different ways. As you become more comfortable, expand your vocabulary by incorporating advanced rudiments like flams, drags, and ratamacues.

The goal is to mix and match rhythmic phrases to create interesting and dynamic solos.

SOLOING TECHNIQUES

One effective soloing technique is **linear drumming**, where no two limbs play simultaneously. This creates a more open and syncopated feel, allowing each note to stand out. For example, you might play a pattern where the bass drum, snare drum, and hi-hat are played in sequence, with no overlap between them. Linear drumming can add complexity and groove to your solos, making them more engaging for the listener. Another common soloing technique is **trading fours and eights**, which involves alternating four or eight bars of soloing with the other musicians in the band. This back-and-forth exchange is a jazz and blues improvisation staple, allowing the drummer to showcase their creativity while maintaining a connection with the band. To practice this, start by trading fours or eights with a metronome or backing track, gradually increasing the complexity of your fills and rhythms.

IMPROVISATION EXERCISES

Engage in regular **improvisation exercises** to improve your skills. One effective method is to **improvise with backing tracks**. Choose backing tracks that suit the style of music you want to improvise in, whether it's jazz, rock, or funk. As you play along, focus on maintaining a groove while experimenting with different rhythms and fills. Another valuable exercise is to **record and analyze your solos**, identifying areas for improvement. Pay attention to your timing, dynamics, and how well you develop your ideas throughout the solo.

When the moment is right in my performances with my band, trading fours or eights is exceptionally cool because it allows each instrumentalist to have their moments of improvisation. I've noticed over the years that the best drum solos 'suspend' time without losing the beat.

You might play triplets or a three-bar measure against a five-bar measure, never losing your place in the sequence of the four or eight measures you're given. Audiences love this, especially when the band knows exactly when to come back in.

SECTION THREE
EXPRESSIVE PLAYING AND DYNAMICS

DYNAMIC CONTROL

Playing with dynamics means transitioning smoothly between loud and soft passages, dramatically changing the mood and energy of a piece.

Accents involve playing specific notes louder than others within a pattern, emphasizing specific beats and creating rhythmic interest. For example, accenting the backbeat (usually on beats two and four) with a strong snare hit can drive the music forward in a standard rock beat.

Ghost notes are very soft, almost inaudible notes, typically played on the snare drum, adding subtle texture and complexity to the rhythm. These quieter notes are usually interspersed between the main beats, giving the groove a more intricate, layered feel.

EXPRESSIVE TECHNIQUES

Playing with dynamics is not just about varying volume; it's also about conveying emotion and playing with feel. Drummers can express emotions like joy, sadness, or tension through their playing by adjusting their dynamics and articulation. For instance, a drummer might play a soft, gentle groove to create a calm, introspective atmosphere or use aggressive, accented strokes to convey intensity and power. Expressive techniques include the use of subtle tempo fluctuations, delicate touch on the cymbals, or the use of space and silence to build tension.

Developing the ability to play with feel requires a deep understanding of the music and a sensitivity to how each note and beat emotionally impacts a performance. If you don't use expressive techniques to enhance your playing in my band, I might as well just use a drum machine.

PLAY TO THE GENRE

Each genre has a flow from verse to chorus. On a power ballad, for instance, a drummer may play a very sparse verse and then use a powerful, expressive tom fill to lead into a strongly played chorus.

Swing and jazz demand an entirely different approach. To play a swing tune from verse to chorus, a drummer often uses a technique called "feathering the bass drum" combined with "ride cymbal patterns" and "accenting the backbeat" on the snare.

•**Feathering the Bass Drum:** The drummer lightly plays the bass drum on all four beats, creating a subtle foundation that maintains the swing feel without overpowering the other instruments.

•**Ride Cymbal Patterns:** The ride cymbal typically plays a "spang-a-lang" pattern (quarter note followed by two eighth notes) that drives the swing rhythm and keeps the time steady.

•**Accenting the Backbeat:** To transition from the verse to the chorus, the drummer might accent the backbeat (on beats 2 and 4) more heavily on the snare, adding energy and emphasizing the shift to the chorus.

Additionally, you could use fills or set-up hits leading into the chorus to signal the change and create a smooth, dynamic transition between sections. These fills often involve the snare, toms, and crash cymbals to build excitement and drive the music forward.

PRACTICAL EXERCISES

Start by playing single strokes on a snare drum, gradually increasing and decreasing the volume with each stroke. This helps develop control over the intensity of each hit. Another effective exercise is to practice rudiments like paradiddles or double-stroke rolls at varying dynamic levels, accenting different strokes to create contrast. To work on expressive drumming, choose pieces that require a wide range of dynamics and emotional expression. For example, practicing ballads or jazz standards incorporating soft, subtle passages and loud, energetic sections can help drummers refine their expressive techniques. Additionally, playing with recordings of expressive drummers, such as **Steve Gadd** or **Vinnie Colaiuta,** can inspire and help you understand how to convey emotion through your drumming. Listen to the music and match the dynamics of any given moment.

DO NOT OVERPLAY

Several years ago, my friend **Wayne Boyer** was performing with a trio in the lounge at a major resort in Palm Desert, California. His drummer was very young and promising, but he had not yet learned the nuances of playing what is called for in each song, so he overplayed everything.

It was fun to watch but very annoying for the other musicians on stage and the audience members who understood the music well enough to realize that the drummer was playing too many notes. We had an expression when that happened with a musician, *"He needs to go to Notes Anonymous!"*

On one particularly slow night, during a break, **Wayne** and the drummer decided to do an arm-wrestling contest at the bar just for fun, and **Wayne** accidentally broke the young drummer's arm!

Wayne felt guilty and did not want his friend to lose work, so the very next night, the young drummer was back on-stage drumming with one arm in a cast, and his performances instantly became perfect! He no longer could overplay, and he fit right in. Hopefully, you won't have to break an arm to know not to overplay! Remember what legendary drummer **Steve Gadd** said:

"Fills bring the thrills, but grooves pay the bills."

Steve Gadd
Credit – Wikimedia Commons

CHAPTER FIVE
RECORDING AND PERFORMING
ARTIST SPOTLIGHT
JOHN BONHAM

"John Bonham, probably the greatest drummer ever – all of us wanted to play drums like him." – Vinnie Paul

Sometimes, one moment or a single recording session can change the trajectory of a genre in music. **John Bonham**, the legendary drummer of *Led Zeppelin*, was a rare example of this phenomenon. His first recording session with *Led Zeppelin* happened in October 1968 at **Olympic Studios** in London while recording their first album, *Led Zeppelin*. This session was the moment that changed **Bonham's** career. Before joining *Led Zeppelin*, **Bonham** already had a reputation as a talented drummer in Birmingham. He seized the moment when guitarist **Jimmy Page** recruited him for his new band. During the recording of *Led Zeppelin*, **Bonham's** speed, power, and technical precision drumming on *"Good Times Bad Times"* and *"Dazed and Confused"* immediately set him apart from other drummers and made him a fan favorite.

The impact of this recording session on **Bonham's** career was profound. *Led Zeppelin* quickly became a massive success, and **Bonham's** drumming was a huge element in the band's groundbreaking sound. His work on the album not only established him as a force to be reckoned with but also as a pioneer in rock music, earning him widespread acclaim. *Led Zeppelin* was an intense band, and **John Bonham** matched that intensity with his performances on stage and in the studio. **Bonham** continued to innovate and push the boundaries of rock drumming until his untimely death in 1980. His first recording session with *Led Zeppelin* launched his career. The intensity and emotion of his performances influenced generations of drummers who continue to look up to him as a pioneer in rock music. He seized the moment and ran with it.

John Bonham
Credit – Wikimedia Commons

"I think every drummer wants to play loud. But you've got to learn to play soft too, you know? When you play with feeling, the notes come out from the heart, and they come out naturally." – John Bonham

SECTION ONE
RECORDING TECHNIQUES

EQUIPMENT AND ACOUSTIC TREATMENT: When it comes to drum recording, whether you're in a home studio or a professional one, a quality drum kit, drumsticks, a variety of microphones (dynamic, condenser, and ribbon mics), an audio interface, a digital audio workstation (DAW), and a set of studio monitors or headphones for accurate playback are all essential.

But it's not just about the gear-acoustic treatment is equally important. Both home and professional studios benefit from bass traps, acoustic panels, and diffusers to minimize unwanted reflections, control low-end frequencies, and ensure a balanced sound. Even simple measures like using rugs or carpets under the drum kit in a home studio can make a difference, reducing room echo and decoupling the drums from the floor. In a professional studio, the room is often treated specifically for drum recording.

MICROPHONE PLACEMENT: In both home and professional studios, start by placing a kick drum mic inside the bass drum, about halfway between the beater and the resonant head, angled slightly toward the point of impact. A snare drum mic should be placed a few inches above the snare drum, angled toward the center of the drum to capture the snap and crack of the snare.

For the toms, use dynamic microphones positioned just above the drumheads, angled toward the center of each tom. Overhead mics are extremely important for capturing the overall sound of the kit, including cymbals; place them in a spaced pair or X/Y configuration about 2-3 feet above the kit, equidistant from the snare drum to maintain stereo balance. A room microphone placed several feet away from the kit can capture the room's ambient sound and add depth to the recording.

Different miking techniques can be employed depending on the desired sound. The **Glyn Johns** technique, for example, uses three microphones: one overhead mic placed above the snare, another overhead mic positioned to the side of the floor tom, and a kick drum mic. This technique captures a balanced, natural sound with minimal phase issues.

Another approach is the **close-miking** technique, where each drum and cymbal has its dedicated mic, allowing for greater control during mixing. However, close miking requires careful attention to phase alignment and mic placement to avoid unwanted phase cancellation.

I prefer the **close-miking** technique, but it takes enormous work and tweaking to get it right. The best scenario is to put your drums into a tracking room where they are not moved (except when switching out specific drums to capture a different sound). Over a short period, you can eliminate most unwanted pickup from other mics and have a killer studio drum sound.

EDITING AND MIXING DRUM TRACKS: After recording, begin by editing the drum tracks, ensuring each hit is in time with the song's tempo. Use tools like quantization to correct timing issues, but be cautious not to over-quantize, as this can result in a robotic sound. Clean up any unwanted noise or bleeding between tracks and consider using drum replacement or reinforcement software to enhance specific drum sounds if needed.

Suppose you used pickups on your drums, as described in a previous chapter. In that case, you can switch out sounds using the midi file generated from the pickup on each drum, assuming you've recorded the midi performance separately.

I've also painstakingly used audio files to replace a snare sound or a kick, replacing each kick or snare individually with a perfect one.

If you use this approach, ensure the replacement drums are properly accented and don't all sound alike.

When mixing drum tracks, set the levels of each drum and cymbal to create a balanced mix. The kick and snare drum are usually the foundation, so ensure they are prominent in the mix. Use EQ to carve out space for each element; for example, boost the low-end frequencies of the kick drum, cut mid-range muddiness on the snare, and add high-end sparkle to the cymbals.

Most EQ plugins nowadays have presets for each drum. Compression can be applied to control dynamics and add punch, particularly on the kick and snare. Consider using parallel compression to blend a heavily compressed version of the drum mix with the original to add depth and sustain without losing the natural dynamics. Finally, add reverb or delay to the room or overhead mics to create a sense of space and ambiance, adjusting the settings to fit the style of the music.

When it comes to panning, I have a personal technique that I find works well. I like to pan the drums as if I was looking at the drum set. The kick drum is panned to the center. The snare is slightly center-left and the hi-hat is slightly center-right. The toms and cymbals are appropriately individually panned left to right as you would find them on the set. A pair of overhead mics and a well-placed room mic rounds out the "room feel" of the sound.

If you're programming drums, check the keynote assignments for each set, and quantize the programmed drums to feel so they don't sound robotic, unless you're going for that vibe. Many tools exist in all major DAW platforms.

Hal Blaine and **Russ Kunkel** are two of the most prolific recording drummers you may have never heard of. **Hal** was the first-call drummer of the famous *"Wrecking Crew"* studio group of musicians in the 1960s and early 1970s. **Russ Kunkel** was the first-call drummer of the famous *"Immediate Family"* studio and live concert group of musicians in the 1970s and 1980s primarily. These two drummers are responsible for hundreds of hit recordings and created popular styles and fills that still resonate in modern drumming. For a course in modern popular drumming technique and playing to each popular genre you are given, study the recordings of **Hal Blaine** and **Russ Kunkel.**

SECTION TWO
PREPARING TO PERFORM

Preparing for a performance is as much about mental readiness as it is about physical preparation. My old friend, **President Gerald R. Ford** said:

"Tell the truth, work hard, and come to dinner on time."

The idea is to keep it all together, and the best way to stay on track is through great preparation.

President Gerald R. Ford and Tad Sisler
Source – Sisler Private Collection

STAGE FRIGHT is a common challenge for many drummers, especially before important performances. To overcome this, harness the power of visualization. Picture yourself performing confidently on stage, playing through your entire set without any mistakes. Envision the audience responding positively and imagine your sense of accomplishment after a successful performance. This mental rehearsal is a potent tool that builds confidence and reduces anxiety. When I first started as a solo performer, I would sit in my car before the gig and pray for the strength to face these people.

As it turned out, most people were encouraging and nice, and I gained confidence naturally through each performance.

BREATHING EXERCISES are excellent for managing nerves. Before going on stage, practice deep breathing: Inhale slowly through your nose. Hold your breath for a moment. Exhale slowly through your mouth. This helps to calm your nerves, steady your heart rate, and focus your mind.

PERFORMANCE PREPARATION

Effective performance preparation starts with thorough rehearsals. Rehearse regularly in the weeks leading up to your performance, focusing on the setlist you'll be playing. Practice playing through your entire setlist without stopping, simulating the performance as closely as possible. Rehearse in a space like the venue to get accustomed to the acoustics and stage setup. Pay attention to transitions between songs, and work on any tricky sections that might cause problems during the performance. When it comes to setlist creation, arrange your songs to maintain energy and engage the audience. Start with a strong, upbeat song to grab the audience's attention, and vary the tempo and intensity throughout the set to keep things interesting.

Consider the set's flow—avoid placing too many similar songs back-to-back, and end with a powerful song that leaves a lasting impression. Make sure to practice the setlist in the exact order you plan to play it, as this will help you get comfortable with the transitions and pacing of the performance. When we were hired to entertain audiences with upbeat music, we had a typical first setlist with my band. We would start with a showstopper, then go right into a straight rock tune, then a power ballad, then usually a medium shuffle-rock piece, and back to three or four dance songs in a row with different beats and tempos before another ballad. Sometimes it wouldn't work that way, and we would scan the audience and adjust to what they most responded to.

"I meet hundreds of people, and I'm not going to remember them. But every single one of them will remember their interaction with me."
— Daniel Radcliffe

Daniel Radcliffe
Credit — Wikimedia Commons

STAGE PRESENCE - AUDIENCE INTERACTION

Drummers can play an active role in engaging with the audience, even from behind the kit. Developing a solid stage presence means exuding confidence and energy while performing. Smile, make eye contact, and show that you enjoy the performance. Even though drummers are often seated, body language is still important—move with the music, using facial expressions to convey your emotion. This connection with the audience can make your performance more engaging and memorable.

Audience interaction is great when you can pull it off. While the lead vocalist usually takes the primary role in engaging the crowd, drummers can contribute by adding excitement to the performance through dynamic playing, using dramatic drum fills, or even interacting with the crowd during breaks between songs when it is called for.

For instance, stand up and acknowledge the audience during a pause, or play a short, energetic solo that gets the crowd clapping. The goal is to make the audience feel like they're part of the performance, creating a memorable and enjoyable experience for everyone involved.

As time passes, you'll be able to read diverse audiences more and make the right calls. The main thing is to enjoy the experience and show it. Remember, the more you enjoy your performance, the more your audience will too. Give them something to remember.

SECTION THREE
PERFORMING LIVE

SOUND CHECK TIPS
Before a live performance, sound check to ensure your drum kit sounds balanced and cohesive with the rest of the band.

During the sound check, individually set the levels for each part of the drum kit.

Work closely with the sound engineer, as their expertise is invaluable in ensuring the kick drum, snare, toms, hi-hats, and cymbals are audible without overpowering one another. Balance the kit so that every element can be heard distinctly on stage and in the audience. After setting individual levels, play through a few songs with the full band to fine-tune the overall mix, ensuring that the drums sit well within the band's sound. Check the levels from different positions in the venue to understand how the kit will sound to the audience.

PLAYING WITH A CLICK TRACK
During the live performance, playing with a click track is one of the best ways to maintain consistent timing. A click track provides a steady tempo guide through in-ear monitors or headphones, helping you stay in sync with the band. This is especially important for complex arrangements or when playing with backing tracks. Practice playing with a click track during rehearsals to get comfortable with it before the live performance. Many of my band performances are heavily sequenced, with recorded music playing behind the band. A click track in the drummer's ear ensures the band is correctly synced to background music. It's ok to use tracks. In today's world, sounding as much like the record as possible only helps in most instances.

MONITORING SOUND
Another important aspect of live performance is monitoring sound on stage. It is not just about hearing your drumming but also about hearing the rest of the band clearly.

If the on-stage sound needs to be clarified, feel free to ask the sound engineer to adjust the monitor mix. Proper monitoring is the key to staying locked in with the other musicians, ensuring a tight, cohesive performance. If you're using in-ear monitors, ensure they're correctly balanced so you can hear your drums and the rest of the band evenly.

I was at a seminar and heard a talk by **Stewart Copeland**, the iconic drummer for the *Police* who became a successful film composer. **Stewart** mentioned that the *Police* performed for three nights at a huge stadium. On the afternoon after the first performance, **Stewart** went in for a sound check, and the monitor blasted in his ears right after the first note. **Stewart** yelled at the sound engineer, ***"Are you trying to make me deaf?"***. The sound engineer apologized, but he told **Stewart** that the monitor was at the exact same level Stewart had asked him to set it during the live performance the night before. **Stewart** realized that it was his own fault, and if he continued to perform at this level, he would most likely lose his hearing, so he left the band and began his new career as a composer.

Sound monitoring is important, and keeping your monitor volume in check is even more critical.

"Drummers shouldn't just think of themselves as drummers. If you're going to be a musician, you should expand your horizons, compose things, and work with other instruments." – Stewart Copeland

Stewart Copeland
Credit – Wikimedia Commons

ANALYZING PERFORMANCE AND FEEDBACK

After the performance, conduct a **post-performance review**. If possible, record the performance so you can analyze it afterward. Listen for areas where your timing, dynamics, or transitions could be improved. Pay attention to how well you maintained energy throughout the set and how effectively you communicated with the band and audience. This self-analysis, under your control, will help you identify areas for improvement in future performances.

In addition to self-review, seek feedback from fellow band members, sound engineers, and trusted audience members. Use this feedback constructively to fine-tune your approach to live drumming. Every live show is an opportunity to learn and grow as a musician.

CORPORATE EVENTS: Performing at corporate events, private parties, weddings, and special occasions with a band can be a lucrative way to make money on a full-time basis. Agencies, companies, and individuals hire musicians to provide live entertainment for their events, offering opportunities for paid performances and networking with potential collaborators and clients. When I started out doing this, I hooked up with an agent who controlled the corporate entertainment of several of the large hotels and convention centers in my area. Because of the number of conventions and private events agents booked for me regularly, I could quit my regular gig and work full-time doing corporate and private parties. It was a lot of setting up and breaking down my equipment. Every night was a different vibe, and I also worked many day events. The financial security and variety of opportunities are advantageous.

HOW TO HANDLE CORPORATE EVENTS: Create a checklist of all equipment, instruments, wires, stands, microphones, speakers, computers, and anything else you need for the gig. You don't want to show up without an essential instrument or stand. Eventually, you'll only need a mental checklist. After breaking down our equipment at the end of each gig, we do what we call the "idiot check," going back and checking around and under the stage for anything we might have missed.

Early arrival at events is crucial. It not only provides you with sufficient time to set up your equipment and address any unforeseen issues but also reassures the event planner. Remember, people tend to arrive early, so be ready to perform at least 15 minutes before your scheduled start time.

Watch your volume, especially during cocktail hours and dinner sets when people like to talk. Always look your best. Grooming and proper dress are essential for corporate gigs. Be accommodating and classy. Attitudes and emotions power everything you do. Do not eat food or drink alcohol unless the client specifically approves it. Always choose appropriate music for the moment.

Make sure your drum set is clean and polished. I know a few drummers that would literally throw their drums in the back of their pickup truck and the drums and hardware would bounce around in the truck on the way to the gig. Their drums always looked scratched and chipped, as if they had come right from a yard sale to the gig. How you present yourself is a direct reflection on you, and this includes your equipment.

Don't take long breaks unless it fits within the client's schedule. I was working a nightclub gig with a trio in **Palm Springs,** and it was a prolonged night, so we took an exceptionally long break. My saxophonist Pat **Rizzo** looked at me and said, *"We'd better go back and play. It's almost time for our next break!"* I loved that joke, but I promise clients and bar owners always look at the time and expect you to take regular breaks. Most musicians play sets of 45 minutes to an hour. The usual break time is fifteen minutes. I've done nights where the client asked in advance for continuous music without breaks, and that's what they get from me. I charged accordingly.

A DIFFERENT DRUMMER

Henry David Thoreau coined the idea of marching to the beat of a different drummer when he said:

"If a man does not keep pace with his companions, perhaps it is because he hears a different drummer. Let him step to the music which he hears, however measured or far away."

Henry David Thoreau
Credit – Wikimedia Commons

You can make money performing and recording on drums. When you perform at corporate events and private parties, you are working within a very structured environment. Most nightclubs allow you a bit more freedom in your performance, letting you 'rock out' or play advanced solos if the gig calls for it.

My approach has always been to paint outside the lines whenever I can. Think outside the box. The greatest musicians can hear something slightly different than others might and elevate a song or a track by their innovative performance. Be that different drummer. Learn as much advanced theory as you can, so you can draw upon great knowledge as you create your own style.

CHAPTER SIX
ADVANCED MUSIC THEORY FOR DRUMMERS

SECTION ONE
ADVANCED RHYTHM

COMPLEX TIME SIGNATURES such as 5/4, 7/8, and 9/8 add a layer of intricacy to a drummer's playing and are often found in genres like jazz, progressive rock, and classical music.

•**5/4 Time Signature**: This signature divides each measure into five beats, creating an unconventional rhythm that can be grouped in different ways, such as 3+2 or 2+3. To practice, start by playing a simple groove in 4/4, then add an extra beat to create a 5/4 pattern. This will help you get accustomed to the asymmetry of the time signature. Check out the song *"Take Five"* by **Dave Brubeck**.

•**7/8 Time Signature**: In 7/8, each measure is divided into seven eighth notes. Common groupings include 4+3 or 3+4. Practice by playing a groove in 4/4 and then adjusting it by removing an eighth note, creating the feel of 7/8.
Over time, you'll develop a natural sense of this rhythm. Study the song *"Money"* by **Pink Floyd** to get the feel of 7/8.

•**9/8 Time Signature**: Typically used in compound time, 9/8 is often grouped as 3+3+3 or 2+2+2+3, and it has a flowing, triplet-based feel. Practice by playing triplets across the drum kit while counting out the nine beats to develop your comfort with this signature. *"The Ocean"* by **Led Zeppelin** features sections using a 9/8 time signature.

POLYRHYTHMS AND CROSS-RHYTHMS

Polyrhythms involve playing two or more conflicting rhythms simultaneously, adding a rich, complex texture to your drumming. This technique is great for Afro-Cuban, jazz, and progressive rock.

•**Defining Polyrhythms**: A common example of a polyrhythm is playing three notes against two (a 3:2 polyrhythm), where one limb plays three evenly spaced notes while another plays two. This creates a syncopated, interlocking rhythm that challenges your coordination.

•**Practicing Cross-Rhythms**: Cross-rhythms occur when two different rhythms are superimposed, but not necessarily in sync.
For example, you might play a steady 4/4 pattern on the bass drum and a syncopated rhythm on the snare or hi-hat. Start with simple exercises, like playing eighth notes with one hand and triplets with the other, gradually increasing the complexity as you become more comfortable.

ADVANCED SYNCOPATION TECHNIQUES

Syncopation is the deliberate disruption of the regular flow of rhythm, often by placing emphasis on off-beats or weaker beats. Mastering syncopation adds a dynamic and unpredictable quality to your drumming.

•**Syncopated Rhythms**: To practice syncopation, start by playing a basic groove, then experiment with shifting snare or kick drum hits to the "and" of the beat (e.g., the off-beats in a 4/4 measure). This creates a more complex, driving rhythm that adds energy and excitement to your playing.

•**Practical Applications**: Apply syncopation by incorporating it into your fills, transitions, and solos. Practice with a metronome, emphasizing the off-beats and varying the dynamics to create different textures. Over time, syncopation will become an integral part of your drumming vocabulary, allowing you to add subtlety and sophistication to your performances.

My friend **Sergio Mendes** had countless multi-platinum hits over decades. His Latin-infused polyrhythms influenced generations of musicians. Sergio served as a cultural ambassador for Brazil, and he got a star on the walk of fame. Still, he remained humble and continued to innovate, collaborating with modern hip-hop artists on his album *"Timeless."* Take **Sergio's** example and continue to explore and diversify your knowledge over multiple genres.

Sergio Mendes and Tad Sisler
Source – Sisler Private Collection

USING TWO KICK DRUMS

Adding a second kick drum to a drum set can open new possibilities for drummers, especially in speed, power, and rhythmic complexity. To set it up, you'll need a second bass drum that matches your primary kick drum in size and tuning (for consistency) or a slightly different size if you want a contrasting tone. Position the second kick drum symmetrically to your main one. Adjust the pedal height and distance to make sure both pedals feel comfortable. Or, you can opt for a double kick pedal, where a single bass drum has two beaters controlled by two pedals. This setup requires less space and maintains a balanced kit look, allowing rapid kick patterns.

Many famous drummers have used two kick drums. **John Bonham** of *Led Zeppelin* was known for his powerful bass drum work, even experimenting with two kicks for a fuller sound. **Neil Peart** from **Rush** also used two kick drums, adding to his already extensive drum kit, allowing him to create complex, polyrhythmic grooves. **Lars Ulrich** from **Metallica** and **Dave Lombardo** from **Slayer** are other iconic drummers who have used two kick drums to play lightning-fast, heavy beats, which work great in metal music.

Additionally, some bands have used two drummers in their lineup, creating a richer and more layered rhythm section. The **Allman Brothers Band** famously used two drummers, **Butch Trucks** and **Jai Johanny "Jaimoe" Johanson**, and these players were great at intricate polyrhythms and a deep groove, adding to their Southern rock sound. The **Grateful Dead** featured **Bill Kreutzmann** and **Mickey Hart**, known as the "Rhythm Devils," and their dual drumming brought a unique, improvisational rhythm to the band's performances. Modern bands like **King Gizzard & The Lizard Wizard** and **The Doobie Brothers** have also utilized two drummers, adding a dense, dynamic rhythm to their live performances.

Incorporating a second kick drum or using two drummers in a band is a great way to create a more powerful and multifaceted sound, enabling drummers and bands to push creative boundaries and explore complex rhythmic landscapes.

SECTION TWO
HARMONY

Music is math. Theory and harmony provide the foundation for a greater understanding of music, just as Geometry does to architecture and Calculus to computer programming.
The knowledge you gain provides a benchmark for critical thinking. You use it in more ways than you would ever imagine without knowing it!

BASICS OF HARMONY

Developing a basic understanding of **harmony** can greatly enhance musicality and the ability to collaborate effectively with other musicians. Harmony combines different musical notes played simultaneously, creating chords and harmonic progressions.

Chord Structures: Chords are the heart of harmony, made up of multiple notes played together. Common chord types include major, minor, diminished, and augmented, each with a distinct sound. Understanding these chords helps you anticipate changes in the music and align your playing with the harmonic structure.

Harmonic Progressions are sequences of chords that define the harmonic framework of a piece of music. Progressions like I-IV-V or ii-V-I are typical in many genres. By understanding these progressions, you can predict changes in the music and adjust your dynamics, accents, and fills accordingly.

MAKE A DIFFERENCE WITH YOUR BOOK REVIEW
Unlock the Power of Generosity
"When we lift others, we find rhythm together."

I grew up surrounded by music, and even though my main instrument was piano, I was always fascinated by the drums, so I learned everything I could about drums to be a better overall musician. Drumming teaches focus, timing, and the incredible skill of coordinating hands and feet to lock into the rhythm. Over the years, as I worked with some of the best drummers out there, I saw that a great drummer is not just about skill but about the feel and timing that bring music to life.

Would you help someone just like you—curious about playing drums but unsure where to start, or already a great drummer who is always wanting to learn more and continue improving?

My mission is to make learning drums and percussion easy, rewarding, and fun for everyone.

But to reach more people, I need your help.

Most people choose books based on reviews. So, I'm asking you to help a fellow drummer by leaving a review.

It doesn't cost anything and takes less than a minute, but it could change someone's musical journey. Your review could help...

- ...one more person discover the joy of drumming.
- ...one more student feel confident in learning.
- ...one more drummer keep the beat steady.
- ...one more dream come true.

If you purchased my book on Amazon, here's the link to leave your review:

https://www.amazon.com/review/review-your-purchases/?asin=1966258038

Or, you can just scan this QR code to get to the Amazon review page:

If you love helping others, you're my kind of person. Thank you from the bottom of my heart!   **Tad Sisler**

APPLYING HARMONY TO DRUMMING

While you primarily focus on rhythm, you can also apply concepts of harmony to your playing, mainly through drum tuning and melodic drumming.

Tuning Drums to Harmonize: Drums can be tuned to specific pitches that complement the song's key. For example, tuning the toms to the scale's tonic, subdominant, and dominant notes (I, IV, V) can create a more harmonious sound that blends well with the other instruments. This tuning approach is beneficial in genres like jazz, where melodic drumming is more prominent. This tuning is usually used only in recording, because you will play songs in multiple keys during a live performance, and tuning to a different key can make the music sound cacophonous.

Playing Melodically: Create melodic phrases by emphasizing different drums and cymbals to reflect the song's harmonic structure. For example, playing higher-pitched drums or cymbals on higher notes in the chord progression and lower-pitched drums on the bass notes can add a melodic dimension to drumming.

Learning actual Music Theory and Harmony as opposed to Drum Theory can also help you immensely in your growth. For instance, if you want to play the Steel Drums, you need at least a rudimentary understanding of Music Theory and Harmony. I had a great percussionist who bought steel drums and carried them out to a poolside gig in Palm Desert, California. It took him a while to learn to play steel drums because he had to catch up on his Music Theory.

Meanwhile, I ended up either putting on a drum pattern and playing the steel drums while he played percussion, or in a most cringeworthy way I would use my steel drum patch on my keyboard to play intricate steel drum melodies while he faked playing the actual steel drums. Not something I'm proud about, nor would I recommend it for your moral compass.

I felt like we were cheating, although I must admit, it sounded fairly authentic.

PRACTICAL EXERCISES

Harmonic Drumming Exercises: Start by tuning your drums to specific pitches that match the key of a song. Practice playing basic grooves and fills while emphasizing the melodic relationship between the drums. For instance, play a groove where the bass drum represents the root note, the snare represents the third, and the toms represent the fifth and seventh.

Playing with Harmonic Instruments: To deepen your understanding, practice with harmonic instruments like a piano or guitar. Focus on aligning your drumming with the harmonic changes in the music.

Play along with simple chord progressions, emphasizing different drums or cymbals as the chords change. This will train your ear to recognize harmonic shifts and adapt your drumming to enhance the musical experience. These exercises help you to become more versatile and dynamic.

SECTION THREE
TRANSCRIBING

DRUM NOTATION is writing down rhythms, patterns, and beats for drummers to read and play. Unlike standard musical notation used for melodic instruments, drum notation has unique symbols and conventions tailored to the drum kit. Here's a detailed overview:

STAFF AND CLEFS
Five-Line Staff: Drum notation is typically written on a five-line staff, like standard musical notation.
Percussion Clef: Instead of the treble or bass clef, drum notation uses a percussion clef, which looks like two vertical lines and two dots.

NOTE PLACEMENT
Each line and space on the staff correspond to a different drum or cymbal. Here's a typical setup:
Bass Drum: Bottom space or line
Snare Drum: Third space or line from the bottom
Hi-Hat: Top line (with an 'x' notehead when closed and an open circle above when open)
Ride Cymbal: Top space or line (with an 'x' notehead)
High Tom: Second space or line from the top
Mid Tom: Middle line
Low Tom: Second space from the bottom
Floor Tom: Bottom line
Crash Cymbal: Above the top line (with an 'x' notehead)

NOTEHEADS AND STEMS
Standard Noteheads: Used for drums (e.g., bass drum, snare drum).
'X' Noteheads: Used for cymbals (e.g., hi-hat, ride cymbal, crash cymbal).
Stems: Typically, notes with stems pointing down are for the bass drum, while stems pointing up are for the snare and cymbals.

RHYTHMIC VALUES
Whole Note: An open notehead without a stem.
Half Note: An open notehead with a stem.
Quarter Note: A filled notehead with a stem.
Eighth Note: A filled notehead with a stem and one flag.

Sixteenth Note: A filled notehead with a stem and two flags.

These rhythmic values are used to indicate the duration of each note, similar to standard notation.

Mastering advanced rhythmic concepts will give you so very much more confidence than you've ever had before.

Believing in yourself and not letting others tell you what you cannot do is the most important thing you can do. Remember what my friend **Khloe Kardashian** said:

"Keep away from people who try to belittle your ambitions. Never allow anyone to take your spirit away from you."

Tad Sisler with Khloe Kardashian and Robin Dougan
Source – Sisler Private Collection

ADVANCED NOTATION TECHNIQUES

ACCENTS AND GHOST NOTES

Accents: Indicated by a '>' above the note, showing that the note should be played louder.

Ghost Notes: Shown in parentheses, indicating the note should be played very softly.

FLAMS, DRAGS, AND ROLLS

Flam: A small note preceding the main note, indicating a grace note played just before the main note.

Drag: Two small grace notes played quickly before the main note.

Rolls: Indicated by a tremolo marking (three slashes through the stem) showing that the note is a roll.

HI-HAT TECHNIQUES

Closed Hi-Hat: An 'x' notehead.

Open Hi-Hat: An 'x' notehead with an open circle above it.

Pedal Hi-Hat: An 'x' notehead below the staff.

DYNAMIC MARKINGS
pp (pianissimo): Very soft.
p (piano): Soft.
mp (mezzo-piano): Moderately soft.
mf (mezzo-forte): Moderately loud.
f (forte): Loud.
ff (fortissimo): Very loud.

REPEAT SIGNS AND CODAS
Repeat Signs: Indicated by double bar lines with two dots, showing that a section should be repeated.
Coda and Segno: Used to direct the player to different music sections.

READING DRUM CHARTS
Drum charts can be simple with basic rhythms or complex with detailed instructions for each drum and cymbal. Familiarize yourself with the specific setup of the chart and what each line and space represent. Start slow, playing each note accurately. Gradually increase speed as you become comfortable. Focus on keeping time and maintaining a consistent rhythm. Read through the entire chart to understand the structure. Pay attention to repeats, codas, and dynamic markings. Practice transitions between different sections of the chart.

HOW TO TRANSCRIBE DRUM PARTS
The transcription process involves listening closely to a piece of music, writing down the drum parts, and analyzing the drumming techniques. Here's how you can effectively transcribe drum parts: The first step in transcribing drum parts is developing acute listening skills. This involves: Focus on the drum part within the song's context. Pay attention to the rhythms, fills, dynamics, and how the drummer interacts with the other instruments. Use audio editing software to isolate the drum tracks or reduce the frequency of other instruments. This makes it easier to hear the drum parts clearly.

Listen to the section you're transcribing multiple times. Start by getting a general sense of the rhythm and patterns, then focus on details like ghost notes, accents, and dynamics. Identify the piece's tempo and time signature, as this will guide your transcription. If needed, use a metronome to match the tempo.

WRITING DOWN DRUM PARTS
Once you've developed your listening skills, the next step is to write down what you hear: Learn and use standard drum notation, which includes the drum staff, note values, rests, and symbols for different drums and cymbals (e.g., X for hi-hat, circles for ride cymbal).

This ensures that your transcriptions are accurate and understandable to others. Begin by transcribing the main beat or groove. Write down the kick, snare, and hi-hat parts first. Then, add in the fills and any variations. Notate the dynamics (loudness or softness) and articulations (such as accents and ghost notes) to capture the drummer's expressive playing style. Transcribe small sections at a time, such as one bar or one phrase, before moving on to the next. This approach helps ensure accuracy and prevents becoming overwhelmed.

ANALYZING DRUM SOLOS

Drum solos are complex and require careful analysis during transcription. Here's how to approach it: Break down the solo into sections, noting the structure (e.g., introduction, development, climax, and conclusion).

Recognize repeated patterns or motifs and note them in the transcription. Pay attention to critical elements of the solo, such as phrasing, dynamics, and the use of space (rests and pauses). Capture these in your transcription to better understand the drummer's approach. Identify and transcribe specific drumming techniques used in the solo, such as rudiments, polyrhythms, or syncopation. For example, when transcribing a solo by Buddy Rich, note his use of single strokes, rolls, and dynamic control.

BREAKING DOWN FAMOUS SOLOS

Studying and transcribing famous drum solos can provide insight into the styles of legendary drummers. Here are a few examples:

•"Caravan" by **Buddy Rich**: Transcribe the solo section to study **Rich's** use of rudiments, stick control, and dynamic contrasts.

•"Moby Dick" by **John Bonham**: Focus on **Bonham's** use of triplets, powerful bass drum work, and syncopation. Note how he builds intensity throughout the solo.

•"Aja" by **Steve Gadd: Gadd's** solo features complex grooves, linear patterns, and intricate fills. Transcribe this solo to learn how **Gadd** combines technique with musicality.

My old friend **Herb Jeffries** was the first African-American singing cowboy movie star in the 1930s. He had a remarkable musical career in the 1940s and 1950s, with huge hits like *"Flamingo"* with **Duke Ellington**, which sold 14 million copies, and a great rendition of *"Caravan."* Herb lived to the ripe old age of 100. He was a delightful person to know. I hope you'll think of **Herb** when you break down *"Caravan."* **Herb Jeffries** broke the color barrier in film and music. He said:

"The word 'black' means 'a void,' so I have never seen a black man. The word 'white' means 'lack of pigment,' so I have never seen a white man either. There's only one race; The Human Race."

———

As a human being, **Herb** was one of the kindest, most giving men I've ever met.

Tad Sisler with Herb Jeffries
Source – Sisler Private Collection

PRACTICAL EXERCISES. Dedicate a few minutes each day to transcribing small sections of songs or solos. Start with simpler pieces and move on to more complex ones. After transcribing a piece, compare your transcription with published versions (if available) or recordings. Analyze any discrepancies and refine your transcription. Expand your musical vocabulary by transcribing drum parts from various genres, like jazz, rock, funk, and Latin music. This helps you understand the different approaches drummers take depending on the style. Record yourself playing and then transcribe it, to help you understand your drumming style and find ways to improve. Work with other musicians to transcribe a song together. This can provide different perspectives and help you learn from others. Many of my friends use transcription software like *Sibelius* or *Finale*, making the entire process so much easier once you get through the learning curve.

CHAPTER SEVEN
BUILDING A PERSONAL PRACTICE ROUTINE

A study published in *Psychological Science* found that regular, consistent practice significantly enhances skill development. Musicians who practiced daily showed improvement rates up to 52% higher than those who practiced less frequently over the same period.

According to research from *The Journal of Neuroscience*, musicians who regularly practice show increased brain plasticity, improving cognitive functions like memory, problem-solving, and processing speed. This is particularly pronounced in those who practice at least 10 hours weekly.

A study from *The Journal of Motor Behavior* indicated that musicians who practiced regularly developed fine motor skills 60% faster than those who did not maintain a consistent practice schedule.

The *International Journal of Music Education* reported that students who practiced an instrument regularly improved their musical skills and performed better academically. They were 21% more likely to excel in math and science than non-musicians.

A survey by the *Royal College of Music* found that 85% of musicians who practiced regularly reported higher levels of emotional well-being and self-confidence. Additionally, 70% noted improved social skills and collaboration abilities when playing in ensembles or bands.

My sister, **Suzanne Ramsey**, was a trained psychologist and a mental health center director for many years. She told me that she found in many patients that simple stress and burnout were the cause of many mental health issues. Fears, including fear of failure or disappointment, were other leading issues beyond simple depression based upon loss.

Suzanne Ramsey and Tad Sisler
Source- Sisler Private Collection

Learning to sing or play an instrument can help to alleviate many mental health issues, and a recent study in *Science Daily* showed that playing an instrument and learning music have been linked to better brain health in older adults. Learning an instrument has also been shown to lessen the chances of developing Alzheimer's and Parkinson's Diseases.

So, when you're practicing and performing, celebrate the fact that you are helping your body and mind in ways you never imagined while at the same time benefiting your audience with the pleasure of your performance! My sister had many tools to help her patients, and music therapy was among those tools.

SECTION ONE
PRACTICE STRUCTURE

Practicing includes mental exercises. Practice being confident. Practice being accurate. Practice being aware. My dear friend, legendary television actress **Mary Tyler Moore** said it best:

"Take chances, make mistakes. That's how you grow. Pain nourishes your courage. You have to fail in order to practice being brave."

Tad Sisler with Mary Tyler Moore
Source – Sisler Private Collection

Properly structuring practice sessions includes setting clear goals, creating a schedule, and employing effective practice techniques. Here's how a drummer should structure their practice:

SETTING SHORT-TERM GOALS

Focus on specific rudiments like the single-stroke roll, double-stroke roll, and paradiddle. Set a goal to master these at various tempos over a few weeks. Aim to learn and perfect a new drum beat or rhythm pattern each week. For example, work on perfecting a basic rock beat one week and a shuffle groove the next.
Set short-term goals for improving specific techniques, such as finger control or bass drum speed. This might involve daily exercises targeting these areas.

SETTING LONG-TERM GOALS

Over the next few months, work on learning various songs across different genres. For example, if you're a beginner, set a goal to be able to play 10 songs from different genres like rock, jazz, blues, and Latin by the end of the year. Set a goal to be performance-ready for an event, such as a gig, recital, or recording session. This includes mastering the setlist, improving endurance, and refining stage presence. After many years, I still do this every time. Endurance is built up over a period. I have enormous lung capacity, and my diaphragm is huge because I use it to sing every day. You will experience the same phenomenon with your body the more you practice. Over the course of several months, incorporate advanced drumming techniques such as polyrhythms, cross-rhythms, and complex time signatures into your playing.

CREATE A PRACTICE SCHEDULE
DAILY ROUTINES

Warm-up (10-15 minutes): Start each session with a warm-up routine that includes stretching, rudiments on a practice pad, and simple hand and foot exercises to prepare your muscles for more intense practice.

Skill Development (20-30 minutes): Focus on developing specific drumming skills, such as stick control, hand-foot coordination, or practicing rudiments. This part of the practice should be focused and deliberate.

Repertoire Practice (20-30 minutes): Work on learning and refining songs. Begin by playing through pieces you're already familiar with, and then spend time learning new material. Practice both the rhythm sections and the fills.

Cool-down (5-10 minutes): End with a cool-down that might include playing at slower tempos, light stretches, and some relaxed drumming to wind down.

WEEKLY PLANS

Review and Reflect: Review what you've practiced at the end of each week. Reflect on your progress toward your short-term goals and adjust the following week's practice schedule accordingly.

Theme Days: Consider dedicating each day to a different aspect of drumming. For example, Mondays focus on rudiments, Tuesdays on groove and feel, Wednesdays on improvisation, and so on.

Rest and Recovery: Incorporate rest days or lighter practice sessions to prevent fatigue and allow your muscles to recover. This also helps maintain enthusiasm for practice.

FOCUS YOUR PRACTICE

Break Down Sections: Focus on small song sections or a specific drumming technique. Work on it repeatedly until you can play it accurately before moving on.

Eliminate Distractions: Ensure your practice environment is free from distractions. This means turning off your phone, avoiding multitasking, and dedicating your full attention to practice.

Set Specific Goals Per Session: Decide what you want to accomplish in each practice session. This could be mastering a particular fill, improving tempo consistency, or learning a new groove.

SLOW PRACTICE

Reduce Tempo: Start practicing new material slowly in tempo. Focus on accuracy and technique.

Gradually increase the tempo as you become more comfortable.

Metronome Use: Practice with a metronome at a slow tempo to develop timing and consistency. This is particularly useful for complex rhythms or challenging sections.

Detailed Focus: Use slow practice to pay attention to the fine details of your playing, such as stick control, dynamics, and articulation. This will help you play more expressively and accurately at faster tempos.

SECTION TWO
OVERCOMING PRACTICE CHALLENGES

Fatigue is a real thing. The best musicians push themselves and ultimately can face burnout. Iconic rocker **Ted Nugent** said:

"I think you should ride the line between fatigue and chaos. The chaos keeps the energy level and spontaneity maximized, while fatigue is just over the edge, and you should try to avoid it."

Ted Nugent
Credit – Wikimedia Commons

DEALING WITH FATIGUE

Hand, wrist, and foot fatigue are common issues for drummers, especially during long practice sessions or performances. Here are some strategies to effectively manage and prevent fatigue:

PROPER WARM-UP AND COOL-DOWN

Always start with gentle warm-up exercises to increase blood flow to your hands, wrists, and feet. This includes light stretching, slow single and double strokes, and gradually increasing tempo. After drumming, perform a cool-down routine to relax your muscles. Gentle stretches and light hand and foot exercises can help reduce tension and prevent stiffness.

CORRECT TECHNIQUE

Grip and Stroke: To minimize tension, use a relaxed grip and proper stroke technique. Avoid gripping the sticks too tightly and focus on using your fingers and wrists efficiently.

Foot Technique: Use the heel-up or heel-down technique for the bass drum and hi-hat pedals as appropriate. Ensure your foot is positioned correctly to avoid unnecessary strain.

THREE SHORT STRETCHING ROUTINES

I can't stress enough how important it is to maintain your physical health. I know a dozen drummers who had massive physical problems as they got older. Drumming is amazing exercise and requires enormous stamina.

WRIST AND FOREARM STRETCH
Wrist Flexor Stretch
Position: Extend one arm in front of you with the palm facing up.
Action: Use your opposite hand to gently pull your fingers back toward your body, stretching the underside of your forearm.
Hold: Maintain the stretch for **15–20 seconds.**
Repeat: Switch to the other arm.

Wrist Extensor Stretch
Position: Extend one arm with the palm facing down.
Action: Gently pull the back of your hand toward your body using the opposite hand, stretching the top of your forearm.
Hold: Maintain for **15–20 seconds.**
Repeat: Switch to the other arm.

Forearm Rotation
Position: Stand or sit with your elbows bent at 90 degrees, keeping them close to your body.
Action: Rotate your forearms so your palms face up, then down.
Repeat: Do this **10 times** slowly to increase flexibility.

SHOULDER AND UPPER BACK STRETCH
Cross-Body Shoulder Stretch
Position: Bring one arm across your chest.
Action: Use the opposite hand to pull your arm closer to your body gently.
Hold: Maintain the stretch for **15–20 seconds.**
Repeat: Switch to the other arm.

Overhead Triceps Stretch
Position: Raise one arm overhead and bend it so your hand touches the middle of your back.
Action: Use your other hand to push your elbow down gently.
Hold: Maintain for **15–20 seconds.**
Repeat: Switch arms.

Upper Back Stretch
Position: Clasp your hands in front of you with your arms extended.
Action: Round your upper back while pushing your hands forward.
Hold: Feel the stretch between your shoulder blades for **15–20 seconds.**

HAND AND FINGER STRETCH
Finger Flex Stretch
Action: Extend one hand in front of you, palm down.
Stretch: Gently pull each finger upward with the opposite hand.

Hold: Stretch each finger for **5 seconds**.
Repeat: Switch to the other hand.

Thumb Stretch
Action: Extend your hand with fingers straight.
Stretch: Gently pull your thumb back with the opposite hand until you feel a stretch.
Hold: Maintain for **10 seconds**.
Repeat: Switch to the other thumb.

Fist to Fan Stretch
Action: Make a tight fist with one hand.
Stretch: Slowly open your hand, spreading your fingers as wide as possible.
Hold: Keep the fingers spread for **5 seconds**.
Repeat: Perform **10 times** on each hand.

TECHINQUES TO AVOID REPETETIVE STRAIN INJURIES

MAINTAIN PROPER TECHNIQUE AND POSTURE
Ergonomic Setup
Throne Height: To maintain proper posture, set your drum throne to the correct height.
Your thighs should be parallel to the ground or slightly angled downward.
Drum Kit Positioning: Adjust your drum kit to ensure all components are within comfortable reach. Position your throne, snare, toms, and cymbals so you can play with a natural, relaxed posture.
Back Alignment: Sit with a straight back and relaxed shoulders to reduce strain.

Proper Grip
Relaxed Hold: Avoid gripping the drumsticks too tightly; a relaxed grip reduces tension.
Matched vs. Traditional Grip: Choose a natural feeling grip style that allows for fluid movement.

Foot Positioning
Pedal Technique: Position your feet comfortably on the pedals, using ankle motion rather than leg force to prevent knee strain.

TAKE REGULAR BREAKS AND VARY YOUR PRACTICE
Take regular breaks during practice sessions to prevent overuse injuries. A 5–10-minute break every 30-45 minutes can help reduce fatigue. During breaks, perform light stretches or shake out your hands and feet to keep them loose and relaxed. This follows the **Pomodoro Technique**, allowing your muscles to relax and your mind to reset.

During your breaks, do something physically different, such as stretching or light walking, relieving muscle tension and improving circulation while preventing injury. After extended practice sessions or when you've been practicing intensely for several days, take a more extended break (an hour or even a day) to recover fully.

Scheduled Breaks
Rest Intervals: Take a 5–10-minute break every hour of practice to rest muscles.
Micro-Breaks: Briefly relax hands and arms between songs or exercises.

VARY YOUR PRACTICE ROUTINES
Incorporating variety into your practice routine keeps things fresh and engaging, preventing monotony and burnout.

VARYING ACTIVITIES
Alternate Focus Areas: Switch between different techniques (e.g., rudiments, grooves, fills) to avoid overworking specific muscle groups.
Cross-Training: Incorporate other forms of physical activity to build overall strength and flexibility.

Mindful Practice
Listening to Your Body: Pay attention to signs of fatigue or discomfort and adjust accordingly.
Gradual Intensity Increase: Slowly build up practice duration and complexity to allow your body to adapt.

STRENGTHENING AND CONDITIONING
Warm-Up Routine
Light Stretching: Begin each session with the stretching routines outlined above.
Slow Playing: Start with slow tempos to prepare muscles before advancing to faster speeds.

STRENGTH EXERCISES
Hand and Wrist Exercises: Incorporate exercises to strengthen and increase the flexibility of your hands and wrists. This can include using hand grippers and resistance bands and doing specific drumming exercises like paradiddles and finger control drills.
Foot Exercises: Strengthen your foot muscles by practicing foot pedal exercises, calf raises, and other lower-body workouts.
Wrist Curls: Use light weights or resistance bands to perform wrist flexion and extension exercises.
Repetitions: Do **2–3 sets of 10–15 reps** each.

Finger Strengthening: Squeeze a stress ball or use grip trainers to enhance finger and hand strength.

ENDURANCE BUILDING
Continuous Play: Practice playing continuous rhythms for extended periods to build stamina.

Incremental Challenges: Gradually increase the duration and complexity of your practice sessions.

HYDRATION AND NUTRITION
Drink plenty of water to keep your muscles hydrated and functioning optimally. A balanced diet supports muscle recovery and overall health. Choose a diet rich in nutrients.

LISTEN TO YOUR BODY
Pay attention to any pain or discomfort. If you experience persistent pain, stop playing and rest. Don't play through pain. It can lead to more severe injuries. If you have ongoing issues with fatigue or pain, consider consulting a healthcare professional such as a physiotherapist or a musician's health specialist.

My father, **Maynard Lee Sisler**, was a physician specializing in internal medicine. He learned medicine on the spot as a medic on a Navy ship in World War II. Doctors were scarce in the South Pacific, so my father quickly learned to diagnose sailors and do emergency surgery when needed.

Years later, after extensive training in medical school, he told me that the most important thing a doctor can do is to listen to their patients. In their own way, they will tell you what you need to know to help them. I believe it's the same with all of us. We must learn to listen to ourselves and what our body and mind tell us. Most of what is wrong with us can be helped immensely by exercise, eating right, and getting enough sleep.

Maynard Lee Sisler, M.D., F.A.C.P
Source – Sisler Private collection

EQUIPMENT CONSIDERATIONS

Choose drumsticks appropriate for your playing style and hand size. Lighter sticks can reduce fatigue during long sessions. Use shock-absorbing mats under your drum kit to reduce impact and strain on your feet.

ROTATING FOCUS AREAS

Assign different focuses to each day. For example, dedicate Mondays to rudiments, Tuesdays to coordination exercises, Wednesdays to improvisation, etc. This ensures that all aspects of your drumming are being developed regularly. Each week, focus on different musical genres such as rock, jazz, blues, or Latin drumming. Learning diverse styles not only improves versatility but also keeps practice exciting. Regularly introduce new techniques or drumming concepts into your practice. This could be anything from trying different grips to exploring polyrhythms or syncopated beats.

INTERACTIVE PRACTICE

Mix in practice sessions where you play along with backing tracks or recordings. This helps you develop timing and groove within a musical context. Occasionally practice with other musicians or join a drumming group. This helps with timing and coordination and simulates a live performance environment. Utilize apps, digital tools, and online resources to bring variety to your practice. These can offer guided lessons, new exercises, and interactive challenges.

MENTAL RELAXATION

Practice mindfulness or breathing exercises during breaks to clear your mind and reduce stress. This can also help you improve your focus when you return to practice. Step away from your practice space during breaks. A brief change in environment can refresh your perspective and boost creativity when you resume practicing. Instead of practicing, take some time to listen to drumming recordings or watch drumming videos. This passive learning can provide new ideas and inspiration without physical effort.

STAY CONSISTENT BY BUILDING HABITS

Practice at the same time every day to establish a routine. Consistent timing helps form a habit, making staying on track with your practice goals easier. The more structured you are, the calmer you become as you relax into a routine. Start with small, manageable practice sessions and gradually increase their length as the habit becomes more ingrained. Even 10 minutes of daily practice can significantly impact when done consistently. Identify triggers or cues that prompt you to start practicing, such as a specific time of day, a particular location, or following a specific activity. Associating practice with these cues makes it easier to stick to your routine.

ACCOUNTABILITY

Keep a practice journal where you document what you practice each day, your progress, and areas that need improvement. This will keep you accountable and allow you to track your progress over time. Partner with a fellow drummer or musician who wants to improve. Regularly check-in, share progress, and critique each other's playing to stay motivated. I always surrounded myself with musicians who were better than me. Their patience and example made me a much better musician. Share your practice goals and progress with friends, family, or on social media. Making your goals public can create a sense of accountability, encouraging you to stay committed.

SECTION THREE
ENHANCING PRACTICE WITH TECHNOLOGY

Legendary Filmmaker **George Lucas** said:

"The technology keeps moving forward, which makes it easier for the artists to tell their stories and paint the pictures they want."

George Lucas
Credit — Wikimedia Commons

AI is changing everything. By the time you read this, many new developments have already happened. Some of the ideas we're suggesting here may already be obsolete. I promised myself when I was young that I would stay current on technology, and I came up with tape-based recording in the big studios to today, where everything exists on the computer. I'm so excited to see what's coming, and if I had one piece of advice for you, I would tell you to stay current and keep learning for as long as you live. Here's how to leverage valuable apps, online resources, and the latest technological advancements:

USEFUL APPS AND TOOLS

Metronome Apps like **Tempo** and **Pro Metronome** help you keep time with precision. They offer customizable settings, allowing you to practice at different tempos, subdivisions, and time signatures.

Some metronome apps include features like tempo trainers that gradually increase speed, helping you build up your timing and endurance over time.

Tuning Apps like **Drumtune PRO** help you tune your drums accurately. They allow you to tune each drum to specific pitches or intervals, ensuring your kit sounds harmonious. These apps often include pitch detection, making it easier to match the tension across lugs and achieve the desired pitch for each drum.

ONLINE RESOURCES

YouTube offers an abundance of free drumming tutorials, from basic techniques to advanced lessons. Channels like **Drumeo** and **Mike Johnston** provide professional instruction, covering various styles, methods, and exercises. Whether you want to learn a specific song, explore different drumming styles, or get tips on improving your practice routine, *YouTube* has a huge amount of content.

ONLINE COURSES

Platforms like **Drumeo Edge** and **Udemy** offer structured online courses tailored to different skill levels. These courses often include step-by-step lessons, practice routines, and instructor feedback.

Some courses provide interactive features, such as quizzes, assignments, and peer reviews, helping you stay engaged and track your progress.

INCORPORATE TECH INTO PRACTICE

Set up a digital practice space with electronic drums or practice pads connected to your computer or mobile device. This allows for silent practice, making it easier to practice without disturbing others. Using virtual drum kits and software like **EZdrummer** or **Superior Drummer**, you can experiment with different drum sounds and styles, adding versatility to your practice sessions.

Record and Review your practice sessions using software like **GarageBand** or **Ableton Live** to record and edit your sessions. Watching or listening to your recordings helps you analyze your timing, dynamics, and technique, enabling you to make targeted improvements.

NEW DEVELOPMENTS WITH AI

New AI-powered tools like **Moises** and **Yousician** (see our section on AI-powered apps) offer real-time feedback on your drumming. These tools analyze your playing, providing insights on timing and accuracy and even suggesting exercises for improvement. AI can create personalized practice routines based on your skill level and goals, adapting to the difficulty as you progress, challenging and motivating you to improve.

CHAPTER EIGHT
PSYCHOLOGICAL ASPECTS OF LEARNING DRUMMING

B illionaire entrepreneur **Richard Branson** said, *"You don't learn to walk by following rules. You learn by doing and by falling over."* Imagine a toddler getting frustrated while learning to walk. The child may squeal or cry, but they do not give up. Learning to walk becomes an obsession until they finally stumble around like a drunken monkey with a massive smile. When learning to play an instrument, you may also feel enormous frustration at your lack of coordination, just like that infant learning to walk. If you could just put yourself back into that mindset of the toddler, wanting nothing more than to accomplish the task in front of you, you could make it all the way! Here are some tools to help you in your journey:

"You pray for things and accept the blessings when they come, you know? And it is about how you talk to yourself and what you say morning, noon and night about what you want to happen in our life. Some folks call that creative visualization. Other people call it prayer. But it is about that message that you send out there to yourself." — Al Jarreau

Al Jarreau
Credit — Wikimedia Commons

SECTION ONE
BUILDING CONFIDENCE

In Section Two of Chapter Five, I touched on stage fright and gave you some exercises for performance preparation. Here, I delve deeper into the mindset you will need to succeed.

OVERCOMING SELF-DOUBT

I performed at a "New Thought" church for 15 years. Although the services were a spiritual experience, I viewed the experience more as a positive-thinking class than a religious session.

After 15 years, I realized that much of the affirmations they taught had become a part of my life, helping me through hard times and tragedy.

It helps to regularly remind yourself of your strengths and past successes. Replace negativity with positive affirmations, like "I am improving every day" or "I can master this technique." Focus on your progress rather than dwelling on mistakes. Acknowledge small victories in your practice sessions, naturally reinforcing your confidence.

VISUALIZATION TECHNIQUES

Visualize yourself successfully performing challenging pieces or playing in front of an audience. This mental rehearsal prepares your mind for actual performance scenarios, reducing anxiety. Picture the audience's applause and your own sense of accomplishment after a performance. This imagery helps create a positive association with playing and reduces stage fright.

SETTING ACHIEVABLE GOALS

Set Specific, Measurable, Achievable, Relevant, and Time-bound goals. Achieving these goals proves your progress, boosting your confidence. Start with more straightforward goals and gradually increase the difficulty. Each success builds your confidence and prepares you for more complex tasks.

DEVELOPING A GROWTH MINDSET

Understand that every challenge is an opportunity to grow. Approach complex drumming techniques or rhythms with curiosity rather than fear, and view mistakes as part of the learning process.

Regularly challenge yourself with new drumming styles, tempos, or exercises. This constant push helps you break through plateaus and develop a resilient mindset.

LEARNING FROM MISTAKES

Instead of getting discouraged by mistakes, analyze them. Ask yourself how you can improve. This reflection turns errors into valuable learning experiences. Understand that mistakes are not a reflection of your ability but a natural part of the learning process. Each mistake moves you closer toward mastery.

PERSISTENCE AND RESILIENCE

Develop a routine that encourages persistence. The more you practice, the more you reinforce your skills and resilience, leading to greater confidence. Remember your end goals and why you started drumming. Whether it's the joy of playing or the desire to perform, staying connected to your motivation keeps you persistent. My dear friend, iconic actor **Elliott Gould** believed strongly in persistence when he said:

"Quitters don't win, and winners don't quit."

Tad Sisler and Elliott Gould
Source – Sisler Private Collection

ACHIEVING MILESTONES

Divide your long-term goals into smaller, manageable milestones, like asserting a particular rudiment, learning a new song, or performing at an open mic. Create a timeline for achieving these milestones. Having a clear roadmap keeps you on track and motivated.

I managed a restaurant when I was young, and the owner, **Lyman Martin**, created a handbook for waiters and waitresses that he called his roadmap to success. He believed that if you followed the concepts in his handbook, you would excel at the job and perform at a high level. It worked. We had a highly trained, professional staff who knew what they were doing, and they all exuded confidence.

"Be firm, fair, consistent, use common sense, and kick ass!"
- Lyman Martin

RECOGNIZING ACHIEVEMENTS

Every time you reach a milestone, take the time to celebrate. Celebrating reinforces positive behavior, whether it's treating yourself to new drum gear or simply acknowledging your progress. Keep a journal or video log of your progress. This record will not only track your achievements but also serve as a reminder of how far you've come.

REFLECTING ON PROGRESS

Periodically review your progress. Reflect on what you've learned, the challenges you've overcome, and how you've grown as a drummer. Use this reflection to set new goals and plan your next steps.

My friend, President **George H. W. Bush**, created a list of motivating thoughts. I turn to this list occasionally, for inspiration to stay emotionally present and focused:

1. Don't get down when your life takes a bad turn. Out of adversity comes challenge and often success.
2. Don't blame others for your setbacks.
3. When things go well, always give credit to others.
4. Don't talk all the time. Listen to your friends and mentors and learn from them.
5. Don't brag about yourself. Let others point out your virtues, your strong points.
6. Give someone else a hand. When a friend is hurting, show that friend you care.
7. Nobody likes an overbearing big shot.
8. As you succeed, be kind to people. Thank those who help you along the way.
9. Don't be afraid to shed a tear when your heart is broken because a friend is hurting.
10. Say your prayers!!"

President George H. W. Bush, Barbara Bush
and Tad Sisler

Source – Sisler Private Collection

SECTION TWO
COGNITIVE BENEFITS

Learning to play the drums engages the way your brain functions, enhancing memory, focus, and creativity. Here's how:

TECHNIQUES FOR MEMORIZATION

Chunking: Break down complex drum patterns into smaller, manageable parts (chunks) to make memorization easier.

This technique helps you remember sequences by grouping similar elements together.

Association: Link drum patterns with visual or verbal cues, like associating a rhythm with a word or image. This association technique aids in quicker recall of drum parts during practice and performance.

BRAIN EXERCISES

PATTERN RECOGNITION: Drumming involves recognizing and repeating rhythmic patterns, stimulating brain areas responsible for memory and pattern recognition. This exercise strengthens neural pathways and improves overall memory function.

VISUALIZATION: Mentally rehearsing drum patterns or visualizing your hand and foot movements reinforces memory retention. Visualization is a powerful brain exercise that enhances your ability to recall and perform drum sequences accurately. You may have heard of the study of three groups of children: The first group was put on the basketball court and told to shoot as many baskets as possible. The second group was told to just visualize shooting baskets over and over. The third group was told not to even think of basketball. Surprisingly, the second group did almost as well as the first group in shooting basketballs after the exercise because visualization works.

REPETITION AND RECALL: Consistent repetition of drum rudiments and patterns reinforces muscle memory and improves recall speed. The brain becomes more efficient at accessing stored information, leading to faster learning and retention. Some people watch me as I play and sing, asking me how I can do this. I tell them, *"Years of endless repetition, and you can do this too!"* Practice drum patterns at intervals, allowing time between sessions. This spaced repetition technique improves long-term memory retention, ensuring patterns stay ingrained.

IMPROVING FOCUS AND CONCENTRATION

Organize your practice sessions with clear goals and time limits. This focused approach helps you concentrate on specific areas of improvement and maximizes the efficiency of your practice time. During practice, fully engage with the task at hand.

Avoid distractions and immerse yourself in the rhythms, sharpening your focus and honing your ability to concentrate for extended periods. Like "runners high," when you intensely focus on your task, you transcend the world around you and can feel it.

ELIMINATING DISTRACTIONS

Create a practice space free from distractions.

Turn off electronic devices, minimize noise, and ensure your environment is conducive to deep concentration. Practice mindfulness while drumming by staying present in the moment. Focus on each beat's sound, feel, and timing, training your brain to maintain concentration and avoid wandering thoughts.

MINDFULNESS TECHNIQUES

Incorporate deep breathing techniques before and during practice to calm your mind and enhance focus. Controlled breathing helps reduce stress and anxiety, allowing you to concentrate better on your drumming. Treat drumming as a form of meditation by maintaining a steady rhythm and focusing solely on the beats. This practice improves concentration and promotes relaxation and mental clarity.

BOOSTING CREATIVITY

Set aside time for unstructured, improvisational drumming. Allow yourself to experiment with different rhythms and patterns without worrying about making mistakes. This freedom encourages creative expression and helps you discover new sounds and techniques. This exercise also helps open your mind to new possibilities; you will surprise yourself when you're performing later. Push your creative boundaries by improvising in different time signatures or genres. This challenge stimulates creative thinking and helps you develop a unique drumming style.

COMPOSING MUSIC

Compose your drum patterns or entire drum compositions. This exercise enhances your creative thinking skills and helps you apply practical theoretical knowledge. Work with other musicians to create new music. Collaborating on compositions encourages creativity by blending different ideas and perspectives, leading to innovative musical outcomes.

EXPERIMENT WITH SOUNDS

Experiment with multiple drum kits, cymbals, and percussion instruments to discover new sounds. Try altering your playing technique to produce unique tones and textures, stimulating creative exploration. Incorporate electronic effects or unconventional playing techniques into your drumming. This experimentation expands your creative palette and allows you to express yourself in new and exciting ways.

Legendary singer **Tina Turner** said:

"Sometimes you've got to let everything go — purge yourself. If you are unhappy with anything... whatever is bringing you down, get rid of it. Because you'll find that when you're free, your true creativity, your true self comes out."

Tina Turner
Credit – Wikimedia Commons

SECTION THREE
EMOTIONAL AND SOCIAL BENEFITS

Drumming is more than just playing music; it can positively impact your life in many ways.

STRESS RELIEF AND RELAXATION

Drumming has been widely recognized as a therapeutic activity that helps reduce stress and anxiety. The physical act of drumming allows you to release pent-up emotions and tension, calming the mind and body. The rhythmic nature of drumming can also have a meditative quality, helping you focus and achieve a state of flow that is both soothing and mentally refreshing. I live by the beach and see many groups in drum circles performing. It feels like a meditative experience, and most participants come out of the experience feeling more relaxed and focused. Incorporating relaxation techniques, like deep breathing or mindfulness, into your drumming practice can further enhance the stress-relieving benefits. Playing at a slower tempo or using softer dynamics can help you relax and unwind after a long day. Drumming is a great outlet for emotional expression. Whether you're feeling joy, anger, sadness, or excitement, you can channel these emotions into your playing.

BUILDING SOCIAL CONNECTIONS

As I just mentioned, being a drummer opens opportunities to join various music groups, such as bands, ensembles, or drum circles. These groups provide a sense of community and belonging. Playing with others enhances teamwork and communication skills as you learn to listen and adapt to the group dynamics. Attending drumming workshops and clinics offers a chance to learn from experienced drummers and connect with fellow musicians. These events allow you to expand your social circle within the music community. Participating in workshops exposes you to new techniques, styles, and ideas, fostering personal and professional growth.

Performing with other musicians, whether in a band or an ensemble, creates strong social bonds and a sense of camaraderie. The shared experience of rehearsing and performing together builds trust and mutual respect among group members. Additionally, live performances offer the thrill of connecting with an audience, further enhancing the social aspect of drumming.

PERSONAL FULFILLMENT

Drumming allows you to set and achieve personal goals, whether mastering a challenging rhythm, learning a new drumming technique, or performing in front of an audience. These goals provide direction and purpose, driving you to continually improve your skills and reach new milestones in your drumming journey. For many drummers, playing professionally or becoming a skilled musician is a lifelong aspiration. Through dedication and persistence, drumming can help them achieve these long-term dreams, bringing a profound sense of accomplishment and fulfillment. The journey towards reaching these dreams is equally rewarding as you experience growth, learning, and self-discovery. One of the most fulfilling aspects of being a drummer is the ability to share your music with others. Whether performing live, recording music, or teaching drumming, sharing your passion with others creates a deep sense of connection and joy. It allows you to inspire and influence others, contributing to the broader musical community while enhancing your personal fulfillment.

Overall, drumming offers many emotional and social benefits that contribute to a richer, more fulfilling life. Whether you're seeking stress relief, social connection, or personal growth, drumming provides an excellent avenue for achieving these goals. Remember what my friend, U.S. Secretary of State, General **Colin Powell**, said:

"The chief condition on which life, health, and vigor depend on is action. By action, an organism develops its faculties, increases its energy, and attains the fulfillment of its destiny."

Secretary of State, General Colin Powell and Tad Sisler
Source – Sisler Private Collection

CHAPTER NINE
ADVANCED PRACTICE TECHNIQUES AND STRATEGIES

I conic drummer **Neal Peart** from the band **Rush** said:

"It's interesting. I've known quite a few good athletes that can't begin to play a beat on the drum set. Most team sport is about the smooth fluidity of hand-eye coordination and physical grace, where drumming is much more about splitting all those things up."

This should be your focus while advancing, to be able to multitask, to develop coordination between your hands and feet separately yet simultaneously.

SECTION ONE
ADVANCED TECHNICAL EXERCISES

My friend **Ed Genovese** is one of the finest drummers I've worked with and an even better person. Back in the day, I was performing across the street from **Ed's** band, and I would jump over on my breaks and admire how well he played in the pocket, locking in with his bass player with impeccable timing. We did about a hundred gigs together over the years, and he was always a delight to hang with, laying a solid foundation for the band each time. Ed solidified his reputation as a pocket player, so he was always in demand. Another solid pocket drummer I love to watch perform is **Abe Laboriel, Jr.,** who toured with Paul McCartney. It's a joy to work with solid pocket drummers! Also, check out the work of **Steve Gadd, Questlove,** and **J.R. Robinson** to study great pocket players. I've been blessed to work with other great players like **Jay Lewis, Bobby Dominguez, Steve Neilen, Sal Frisaura,** & **Andrew Fraga, Jr.**

PLAYING IN THE POCKET

Playing "in the pocket" is a crucial skill for any drummer, as it involves creating a solid, steady, and cohesive groove that locks in with the other musicians in a band. Here's a comprehensive guide to understanding and mastering this essential drumming concept:

What Does "In the Pocket" Mean?   Playing "in the pocket" means maintaining a consistent, tight groove that perfectly aligns with the rhythm section, mainly the bass player, creating a seamless and driving feel in the music. It involves impeccable timing, subtle dynamics, and a deep understanding of the song's groove, allowing the drummer to blend seamlessly into the music rather than standing out.

KEY ELEMENTS OF POCKET PLAYING

Maintain a constant tempo throughout the song. Use a metronome during practice to develop a reliable internal clock.

Understand and feel the subdivisions of the beat (e.g., eighth notes, sixteenth notes) to maintain precise timing. Sync with the bass player to create a cohesive rhythm section.

Listen to the bass lines and ensure your kick drum patterns complement them. Pay attention to the dynamics within the groove. Subtle changes in volume and intensity can enhance the pocket feel. Focus on the groove rather than flashy fills and complex patterns. Simplicity often results in a tighter pocket. Play fewer notes with greater precision. Make each note count and fit perfectly within the groove. Highlight important beats in the groove, such as the backbeat on 2 and 4. Incorporate ghost notes on the snare to add texture and subtlety without overpowering the groove. Constantly listen to the other musicians. Adjust your playing to complement and enhance their parts. React to the dynamics and phrasing of the other instruments, creating a musical conversation.

EXERCISES TO DEVELOP POCKET PLAYING

Play simple grooves with a metronome at various tempos. Focus on consistency and timing. I solidified my keyboard bass playing by working with a drum machine to play solidly in the pocket when I played keyboard bass in a band when we couldn't afford a bass player. Practice playing grooves with different subdivisions (e.g., quarter notes, eighth notes, sixteenth notes) to internalize the beat. Practice with recordings of bass lines, focusing on locking in with the bass player's timing and groove. Practice with a bass player, working on creating a tight and cohesive rhythm section. Practice incorporating ghost notes into your grooves. Start slowly and gradually increase the complexity. Play grooves at different dynamic levels. Practice transitioning smoothly between soft and loud playing. Work on accenting different parts of the beat within a groove. For example, emphasize the backbeat (beats 2 and 4) while keeping the other notes softer. Focus on playing solid backbeat grooves. Ensure the snare hits on beats 2 and 4 are consistent and robust. Listening to Reggae drummers helps solidify this exercise.

As I mentioned, listen to recordings of drummers known for their pocket-playing. Transcribe and learn their grooves. Practice playing with songs with solid grooves. Focus on blending in and maintaining a steady pocket.

Playing "in the pocket" is more than technical skill; it's about feel, consistent timing, groove, simplicity, dynamics, and musicality.

"A good groove releases adrenaline in your body. You feel uplifted, you feel centered, you feel calm, you feel powerful. You feel that energy. That's what good drumming is all about." – Mickey Hart

Mickey Hart

COMPLEX RUDIMENTS AND PATTERNS

EXTENDED RUDIMENTS: Once you've mastered the basic rudiments like single strokes, double strokes, and paradiddles, it's time to dive into extended rudiments, including advanced patterns like the Ratamacue, Swiss Army Triplets, and inverted paradiddles. Mastering these will give you more nuanced control over your sticks and allow you to quickly execute more intricate drumming patterns. In this section, I'll delve a little further into techniques I've already mentioned, a good reminder to go back and master it all now.

ODD TIME SIGNATURES: Drumming in odd time signatures, like 5/4, 7/8, or 9/8, adds a layer of complexity to your playing. Learning to groove and create fills within these time signatures will broaden your rhythmic vocabulary and make you more versatile as a drummer. Practicing with odd-time signature tracks and gradually integrating these rhythms into your regular practice will help you become comfortable with these complex patterns.
Practice paradiddles in 7/8 or Swiss Army Triplets in 5/4. This will not only challenge your technical skills but also improve your timing and rhythmic feel. Create custom exercises that combine these elements and work on them with a metronome to ensure accuracy.

SPEED AND ACCURACY DRILLS
METRONOME EXERCISES: Precision is key to fast drumming, and using a metronome is essential for developing speed and accuracy. Start slow and gradually increase the tempo. Use the metronome to lock in your timing, focusing on even strokes and maintaining consistent volume between hits.

GRADUAL SPEED INCREASES: Speed doesn't only come after some time; it requires consistent practice. Start with a comfortable tempo and increase the speed by small increments over time. This technique, known as "gradual speed increases," allows your muscles to adapt to faster playing while maintaining control and precision.

Track your progress by setting tempo goals and challenge yourself to beat your previous records. Check out Charlie Parker's version of *"Cherokee"*. If you can master playing with precision at this fast tempo, you've made it! Focus on developing precision by practicing rudiments and patterns with strict attention to detail. Ensure that each stroke is clean and no flamming unless intended. Work on ghost notes and accents, paying close attention to their volume and placement within the groove. Precision drills, where you alternate between ghost notes and accented notes, can significantly improve your control.

HAND INDEPENDENCE EXERCISES
SEPARATE HAND PRACTICE: Practice each hand separately to ensure that both hands are equally strong and capable of executing patterns independently. For example, practice paradiddles or flam patterns with one hand while keeping a steady rhythm with the other. This will help you develop the ability to play different rhythms with each hand simultaneously. Practice exercises that require your hands to play different rhythms while your feet keep a steady pulse or vice versa. For example, practice playing a basic rock beat with your feet while your hands play a syncopated rhythm on the snare and ride cymbal. Over time, these drills will enhance your overall coordination and improve your ability to play complex rhythms.

COMPLEX PIECES: Once you've developed a solid foundation, challenge yourself by learning and playing complex drum pieces that require advanced hand independence. Choose pieces that incorporate polyrhythms, cross-rhythms, and intricate fills. Breaking down these pieces into smaller sections and practicing them slowly before increasing the tempo will help you master even the most challenging parts. Remember, no matter how good you were yesterday, every day gives you a new chance to reinvent yourself and improve. My dear friend, *NFL Hall of Fame* Linebacker **Junior Seau**, said best:

"The past isn't going to get you to your goal."

Tad Sisler with NFL Hall-of-Fame Linebacker Junior Seau
Source – Sisler Private Collection

SECTION TWO
ENHANCING MUSICAL EXPRESSION
DYNAMICS AND ARTICULATION
As an advanced drummer, you should be able to seamlessly transition between soft (piano) and loud (forte) playing and manage the nuances in between, such as mezzo-piano (moderately soft) and mezzo-forte (moderately loud). Practicing dynamic control involves focusing on the volume of your strokes, ensuring that each hit is deliberate and controlled, whether you're playing a whisper-soft ghost note or a powerful accent. Articulations, such as staccato (short and detached) and legato (smooth and connected), can dramatically change the feel of a drum part. Experiment with different articulations on various parts of the kit—such as snare, toms, and cymbals—to discover how they influence a piece's overall sound and feel. Incorporating rimshots, dead strokes, and open versus closed hi-hats into your playing can add a wealth of expressive potential.

EXPRESSIVE TECHNIQUES
Beyond dynamics and articulation, advanced expressive techniques include accents, ghost notes, and cross-sticking to add texture and depth to your playing. Practicing exercises that focus on these elements will help you develop the ability to play with emotion and subtlety, transforming a basic rhythm into a more expressive, musical statement. Just as you breathe and express your feelings, so must your performance.

PHRASING AND INTERPRETATION
A phrase in music is like a sentence in language; it's a complete musical thought. Understanding how to identify and structure phrases in your drumming will enable you to play more musically. Focus on learning when to emphasize specific beats or sections to enhance the piece's overall structure. This understanding will help you create more compelling and logical drum parts. Interpretation involves making choices about how to play a piece of music based on its style, the intentions of the composer, and your personal artistic vision. As an advanced drummer, you should experiment with different interpretations, such as varying the tempo slightly or altering the dynamics to bring out some aspects of the music. This interpretative skill is what separates a technically proficient drummer from an artist. One of the hallmarks of an advanced musician is the ability to inject their personality into their playing. This might mean altering a standard fill, adding unexpected accents, or playing with a different feel. Developing a personal style involves experimenting with various techniques and sounds until you find what resonates most and then consistently apply it to your drumming.

EMOTIONAL CONNECTION

To play expressively, you must first connect emotionally with the music. This connection allows you to convey the intended emotion of a piece to the audience. Practice playing pieces that evoke a strong emotional response in you, and focus on how that emotion influences your dynamics, tempo, and phrasing. The goal is to make the audience feel what you are feeling through your drumming. Drumming is about communicating emotions. Your drumming should reflect these emotions, whether the music calls for intensity, joy, sorrow, or calm. Techniques such as playing softer or louder, varying your tempo, or adding subtle changes in articulation can all contribute to expressing the intended emotion of a piece. Think of your drumming as storytelling, where each beat and phrase contribute to the narrative. Just as a story has a beginning, middle, and end, your drumming should guide the listener on a journey. Use dynamics, phrasing, and emotional expression to take your audience from one emotional state to another, creating a powerful and memorable musical experience.

My friend, legendary *CNN television* personality **Larry King**, said:

"If you do something, expect consequences."

Some might look at that comment negatively, but my take on it is simple: The harder you work at your craft, the more exponential the progress.

Larry King and Tad Sisler
Source – Sisler Private Collection

SECTION THREE
UTILIZING FEEDBACK AND CRITIQUE

SEEKING CONSTRUCTIVE FEEDBACK

A mentor can advise you, share their experiences, and guide you in honing your skills, offering a fresh perspective. Regular sessions with a mentor can ensure you are on the right path to continuous improvement.

Engaging with your peers is another excellent way to gain constructive feedback. Drumming is often a collaborative effort, so discussing performance with other musicians or fellow drummers can provide insights you might have yet to consider. Peer reviews can also help you understand how your drumming fits within a group context, offering a broader perspective on your musical expression.

When you receive feedback from mentors, peers, or even your audience, analyze it carefully. Understand the intent behind the feedback and consider how it aligns with your goals. Look for patterns in your feedback to identify areas needing consistent improvement.

SELF-CRITIQUE TECHNIQUES

Record your practice sessions and performances. Listening back lets you catch details you might miss while playing, such as timing issues, inconsistent dynamics, or unintentional errors. Reviewing these recordings helps you track your progress and make targeted improvements. After reviewing your recordings, note your strengths and weaknesses. Acknowledge what you do well. At the same time, identifying weaknesses allows you to focus your practice sessions on areas that need the most attention, ensuring balanced skill development. Set specific, measurable goals once you've identified your strengths and weaknesses. These goals could include mastering a particular rudiment, improving timing, or enhancing dynamic control.

ADAPTING TO CRITICISM

Instead of viewing criticism as a personal attack, try to see it as an opportunity to improve. Take a step back, assess the validity of the feedback, and think about how you can use it to refine your playing. Developing a thick skin in response to criticism will help you remain open to learning. Remember what **Don Miguel Ruiz** said in his famous book, *The Four Agreements*, *"Don't take anything personally."* Appreciate criticism of any kind and make it constructive. It's the fastest way to grow. Criticism often highlights areas where you can grow the most. Embrace the feedback you receive by incorporating it into your practice routine. For example, if you're told your fills are too predictable, explore new fill patterns or improvisation techniques. By actively learning from criticism, you can turn potential weaknesses into strengths. Every musician has areas they can improve, no matter how advanced. Celebrate small victories. A positive attitude will keep you resilient and driven, even when faced with challenging feedback.

The great motivator **Norman Vincent Peale** said:

"The trouble with most of us is that we would rather be ruined by praise than saved by criticism."

Remember this and embrace feedback!

Norman Vincent Peale
Credit: Library of Congress via Picryl.com

SECTION FOUR
MASTERING PERCUSSION INSTRUMENTS

Most of the great drummers I know are also excellent at percussion.

I've worked with masters of percussion who focus on percussion over drums, including my friend **Dio Saucedo,** who performed with many of the greats, including **George Benson. Dio** and I have done dozens of gigs together, and there's nobody better.

I have other friends who are great classical percussionists in major orchestras. They love what they do, and they make money doing it. A professional drummer should understand percussion instruments and their application and be able to perform proficiently on each instrument if possible. If you're not a total beginner, I hope you'll forgive me for describing the major percussion instruments as if you've never seen one before:

Congas are tall, narrow drums of Afro-Cuban origin traditionally played with the hands. They are typically tuned to different pitches and played in two or more sets.

Genres: Latin, Afro-Cuban, jazz, world music, salsa.

A master percussionist uses congas to drive the rhythm in Latin and Afro-Cuban music, providing the fundamental groove. In salsa, congas form the backbone of the rhythm section, often playing complex patterns that syncopate with other percussion instruments. In jazz and world music, congas add depth and a distinct timbre, often featuring prominently in solos or as part of intricate polyrhythmic structures.

Bongos are two open-bottomed hand drums of different sizes, traditionally played with the fingers. The smaller drum is called the "macho," and the larger the "hembra."

Genres: Latin, Afro-Cuban, jazz, salsa, world music.

Bongos are essential in Latin music for adding syncopation and melodic rhythms. A master percussionist uses bongos to create sharp, high-pitched rhythms that complement the deeper tones of the congas. Bongos often play the "martillo" pattern in salsa, while in jazz and world music, they can be used for more improvised, expressive playing.

Timbales are a pair of shallow, metal-framed drums, usually accompanied by a cowbell and cymbals. They produce a sharp, staccato sound.
Genres: Latin, salsa, mambo, cha-cha, Afro-Cuban, jazz.
Timbales are central to many Latin genres, where they are used by a master percussionist to lead the rhythm section. In salsa and mambo, timbales provide dramatic accents, rolls, and fills that enhance the energy of the performance. The percussionist might also use the timbales' rims and cowbells to create various percussive effects, driving the music forward with dynamic rhythms.

"The thing about playing percussion is that you can create all these emotions that can be sometimes beautiful, sometimes really ugly, or sometimes sweet, sometimes as big as King Kong and so on. And so there can be a real riot out there, or it can be so refined."
– Dame Evelyn Glennie

Dame Evelyn Glennie
Credit – Creativecommons.org via Flickr

Djembe is a rope-tuned skin-covered drum played with bare hands originating from West Africa, with a wide tonal range, producing bass, tone, and slap sounds.
Genres: African traditional music, world music, fusion, jazz.
A master percussionist uses the djembe to create complex, polyrhythmic patterns central to West African music. The djembe can be the lead drum in ensembles, where it drives the rhythm and interacts with other drums and instruments. In world music and fusion, the djembe adds an earthy, organic feel, often serving as the rhythmic foundation or as a solo instrument.

Cajón is a box-shaped percussion instrument. Originating in Peru, it is played by slapping the front or rear faces (usually made from very thin plywood) with the hands or fingers.

Genres: Flamenco, Afro-Peruvian, Latin, acoustic, world music.

The cajón is versatile and used by a master percussionist to create bass and snare drum-like sounds, making it an excellent choice for acoustic performances. In flamenco, the cajón adds a sharp, percussive drive that matches the rhythm of the dance.

It is also popular in modern acoustic settings, where it can replace a full drum kit, providing both rhythm and dynamics in an intimate, unplugged performance.

Maracas are a pair of rattles typically made from gourds or plastic shells filled with seeds or beads, shaken to produce a rhythmic sound.

Genres: Latin, salsa, merengue, cumbia, world music.

A master percussionist uses maracas to add a consistent rhythmic background, often complementing other percussion instruments. Maracas provide the steady, driving pulse in salsa and merengue that supports the music's rhythm. In other genres, maracas can be used for color and texture, subtly enhancing the ensemble's overall sound.

Tambourine is a frame drum with zills, or small metal jingles attached around the frame. It can be played by shaking, hitting, or striking with a hand or stick.

Genres: Rock, pop, classical, folk, gospel, Latin.

A master percussionist uses the tambourine to add brightness and accentuation to the music. In rock and pop, it is often used to emphasize the backbeat or to add energy during choruses. In classical music, the tambourine is used for color and dynamics, while in folk and gospel, it can lead the rhythm or add to the celebratory feel of the music.

Triangle is a small, triangular metal bar struck with a metal rod, producing a high-pitched, ringing tone.

Genres: Classical, orchestral, folk, world music, Latin.

A master percussionist uses the triangle to add a bright, shimmering sound that cuts through an ensemble. In classical and orchestral settings, it often adds subtle rhythmic accents or highlights specific moments in the music. In folk and world music, the triangle can add a light, delicate texture that complements other instruments.

Claves are two short, thick wooden sticks struck together to produce a sharp, clicking sound. They are integral to many Afro-Cuban rhythms.

Genres: Latin, Afro-Cuban, salsa, rumba, world music.

Claves maintain the "clave" rhythm in many Afro-Cuban and Latin music styles. A master percussionist uses claves to establish the fundamental rhythmic pattern that guides the rest of the ensemble. The claves' rhythm is crucial in salsa, rumba, and other genres, supporting the music's structure.

Castanets are a pair of concave wooden shells joined on one edge by a string. They are played by clicking them together with the fingers.
Genres: Flamenco, Spanish folk music, classical.
Castanets are primarily used in flamenco music to add rhythmic intricacy and drive. A master percussionist uses them to match the intensity and rhythm of the dance, often playing complex, fast-paced rhythms that enhance the dramatic effect of the performance. In classical music, castanets might be used to evoke a Spanish atmosphere or to add rhythmic interest.

Glockenspiel is a percussion instrument made from tuned metal bars arranged like a piano keyboard, played with mallets.
Genres: Classical, orchestral, jazz, pop, world music.
A master percussionist uses the glockenspiel to add melodic and harmonic elements to a performance. Classical and orchestral music is often used for bright, bell-like tones that can carry a melody or add a sparkling quality to the ensemble's sound. In jazz and pop, the glockenspiel can be used to create unique, high-pitched melodies or embellishments.

Vibraphone is very much like the glockenspiel. Its resonators are made of metal bars and rotating discs, which produce a vibrato effect when played with mallets. I've recorded many times with master jazz vibraphone players. Check out the work of **Lionel Hampton** and his vibes will blow your mind!
Genres: Jazz, classical, contemporary, fusion.
A master vibraphonist performs both melodic and harmonic roles, often taking on a lead role in jazz ensembles. The vibraphone's unique sound is perfect for smooth, flowing lines and rich chords. In classical and contemporary music, it adds a shimmering texture that can evoke both warmth and mystery.

Xylophone is made of wooden bars arranged like a keyboard, struck with mallets to produce a sharp, percussive tone.
Genres: Classical, orchestral, jazz, world music.
A master xylophonist creates bright, articulate melodies and rhythmic patterns. In classical and orchestral music, the xylophone can add a playful or dynamic quality. It can be used in jazz for intricate solos or to add a distinctive, resonant texture.

Timpani (Kettledrums) are large, tunable drums with a bowl-shaped body. They are typically played in pairs or groups of four and struck with mallets.
Genres: Classical, orchestral, cinematic, contemporary.

A master percussionist uses timpani to add dramatic, powerful musical elements, particularly in orchestral and cinematic contexts. Timpani often emphasizes critical moments with deep, resonant notes, creating tension or grandeur.

They are also used for melodic lines and thematic material, especially in classical compositions by composers like **Beethoven** and **Mahler**. The ability to tune the timpani allows the percussionist to create harmonic progressions and reinforce the tonal foundation of the ensemble. I use a lot of timpani in my film underscore for big moments.

Marimba has wooden bars arranged like a keyboard, struck with mallets to produce warm, resonant tones.
It is like the xylophone but with a richer, deeper sound due to its resonators.
Genres: Classical, jazz, contemporary, world music.
A master marimba player performs melodic and harmonic roles, often playing complex, multi-mallet pieces that showcase the instrument's full range. Classical and contemporary music use the marimba for solo performances, chamber music, and orchestral works. Its rich, mellow tone makes it ideal for creating atmospheric textures or intricate, layered rhythms.

Bodhrán is an Irish frame drum, traditionally played with a wooden stick called a "tipper" or with the hand. It produces a deep, resonant sound.
Genres: Irish traditional music, Celtic music, folk, world music.
A master percussionist uses the bodhrán to drive the rhythm in Irish and Celtic music, providing a pulsating beat that supports the melody. The bodhrán's pitch can be modulated by applying pressure to the drumhead with the non-playing hand, allowing dynamic, expressive playing. It is often used in folk ensembles, interacting with traditional instruments like the fiddle and tin whistle.

Tabla is two hand drums originating in India. It consists of a smaller drum (Dayan) and a larger drum (Bayan), played with intricate finger and hand techniques.
Genres: Indian classical music, Bollywood, fusion, world music.
A master percussionist uses the tabla to perform complex rhythmic cycles, known as "taals," which are fundamental to Indian classical music. The tabla is known for its highly expressive sound and a wide range of tones. In fusion and world music, the tabla adds a unique rhythmic layer that complements other instruments and brings an exotic flavor to the music. **Ed Sheeran** used the table prominently in his pop hit *"Shape Of You."*

Darbuka (Doumbek) is a goblet-shaped drum, traditionally made of clay or metal, played with the hands to produce sharp, staccato sounds.
Genres: Middle Eastern music, belly dance music, world music.

A master percussionist uses the darbuka to create fast, intricate rhythms central to Middle Eastern music. The darbuka is often used in belly dance performances, where its rhythms drive the dance movements. In world music, it adds a distinct percussive voice that can be used both in solo performances and as part of larger ensembles.

Pandeiro is a Brazilian hand-framed drum with a head made of animal skin or synthetic material and jingles (platinelas) around the frame.
Genres: Samba, bossa nova, Brazilian folk music, capoeira.
A master percussionist uses the pandeiro to play the intricate rhythms of Brazilian music, such as samba and bossa nova. The pandeiro's versatility allows the percussionist to simultaneously play the melody and rhythm, often using advanced techniques like finger rolls and slaps. In capoeira, the pandeiro provides the rhythmic foundation for martial arts movements.

Güiro is a Latin American percussion instrument made from a hollow gourd with parallel notches cut into one side. It is played by scraping a stick along the notches. In the studio, we sometimes call this the "fishbone."
Genres: Latin, salsa, cumbia, son cubano.
A master percussionist uses the güiro to add rhythmic texture and syncopation in Latin music.

The güiro's distinctive sound is essential in genres like salsa, where it adds a driving, percussive rhythm that complements the other instruments. The güiro is often used to maintain a steady rhythm throughout the song, contributing to the overall groove and feel of the music.

Shekere is a West African percussion instrument made from a dried gourd covered with a beaded net. It is played by shaking and striking.
Genres: African traditional music, Afro-Cuban music, world music.
A master percussionist uses the shekere to add rhythmic complexity and color to performances. In African traditional music, the shekere often accompanies drums and other instruments, providing a rich, percussive texture. In Afro-Cuban music, it can be used to complement the congas and bongos, adding a unique sound that enhances the overall rhythm.

Chimes, also known as "tubular bells," are a set of tuned metal tubes suspended vertically, struck with a mallet making a bell-like sound.
Genres: Classical, orchestral, cinematic, contemporary.
A master percussionist uses chimes to add a bright, ethereal quality to orchestral and cinematic music. Chimes often highlight key moments in a composition, providing a resonant, majestic sound that can evoke a sense of grandeur or drama. In contemporary music, chimes might be used to add texture and atmosphere, creating a sense of space and depth.

Agogô Bells are a pair of metal bells of different sizes connected by a bent metal rod, played with a stick.

Genres: Samba, Afro-Brazilian music, world music, jazz.

A master percussionist uses agogô bells to create high-pitched, syncopated rhythms characteristic of samba and other Afro-Brazilian genres. The agogô bells are often used in call-and-response patterns, adding a sharp, percussive element that interacts with other instruments in the ensemble.

In jazz and world music, agogô bells can be used to add an exotic, rhythmic flavor.

A master percussionist adapts techniques and rhythms to fit the musical context. From the deep, resonant tones of the congas and timpani to the sharp, staccato sounds of the snare drum and castanets, each percussion instrument offers unique possibilities for expression and rhythm. You can create rich, diverse soundscapes that captivate audiences and elevate the music. A professional drummer who plays these instruments proficiently will further develop their mastery.

INCORPORATING ARTIFICIAL INTELLIGENCE

Use the latest technology to master drums and percussion. Here are some popular AI-powered apps (at the time I'm writing this book) that drummers and percussionists can use to practice, expand their repertoire, perform, and record:

Moises.ai is an AI-driven music practice app that allows users to isolate or remove specific instruments from a song, including drums. It also lets you adjust the tempo and key of tracks. Drummers can use the app to create custom backing tracks by removing the original drum track, enabling them to practice along with a band. The tempo control and looping functions are ideal for working on difficult sections. This app is great for drummers who want to practice with realistic backing tracks, isolate specific parts to better understand rhythms, or prepare for performances.

Yousician offers interactive lessons and real-time feedback for learning various instruments, including drums. It listens to your playing and gives instant feedback on timing and accuracy. The app provides structured lessons, rhythm exercises, and a variety of songs to play along with. This app is great for all levels, from beginners to advanced drummers. This app is ideal for practicing basic rudiments, learning new rhythms, or expanding your drumming repertoire through guided lessons.

Melodics is a desktop app that provides interactive lessons for drummers, focusing on rhythm, timing, and groove. The app features drum pad lessons, finger drumming tutorials, and a growing library of songs to practice with. It offers real-time feedback, helping drummers improve their accuracy and feel.

This app is perfect for drummers who want to practice groove, expand their rhythm vocabulary, and learn new techniques in an engaging, structured way.

Drumtune PRO is an AI-powered drum tuning app that helps drummers tune their drums accurately. The app analyzes the pitch of each drum lug and provides tuning recommendations to achieve a consistent, balanced sound across the drum kit. It also has presets for different drum types and genres. This app can be helpful for drummers who want to improve the sound of their drum kit, whether for live performances or recording sessions.

BeatMirror is an AI-driven metronome app that tracks your tempo as you play in real-time, providing visual feedback on your timing accuracy. The app displays your tempo in beats per minute (BPM) and helps you stay in sync with the beat. It's an excellent tool for practicing consistent timing and groove. This app is ideal for drummers working on timing accuracy or practicing complex rhythms and tempo changes (and who isn't?).

Soundbrenner is an AI-powered metronome app that integrates with a wearable device to help drummers feel the beat through vibrations. It offers customizable metronome settings, including subdivisions, accents, and tempo adjustments. The app can sync with multiple devices for group practice or live performance. This app is also great for drummers who want to practice timing and rhythm, especially when practicing with a silent metronome during live performances or recording sessions.

JamKazam is a platform that allows musicians to play together online in real-time, with low latency. It's especially useful for drummers who want to practice or perform with other musicians remotely. The app provides options for creating online jam sessions, recording performances, and even playing live virtual gigs. In case you're stranded on a desert island with the internet, this app is ideal for drummers who want to collaborate with other musicians from a distance, whether for practice or live online performances.

Superior Drummer 3 is a virtual drum studio with AI-powered features to create realistic drum tracks. It offers advanced sound design and mixing capabilities. The software includes a vast library of drum samples, grooves, and MIDI patterns. It uses AI to assist with groove creation, humanization, and beat detection. This app is perfect for drummers who want to create drum tracks for recording or composition or those looking to expand their skills in music production.

Moog Model D (or Other Drum Synthesis Plugins): Synthesizers and drum synthesis plugins, like the Moog Model D, can create electronic drum sounds and beats. These plugins allow for sound manipulation and beat-making, which can help drummers expand their skills in electronic music production. These plugins are helpful for drummers who want to delve into electronic music or add synthesized drum sounds to their live performances.

LANDR is an AI-powered mastering service that enhances the quality of drum recordings by applying mastering algorithms. The platform provides automated mastering to polish drum tracks and offers distribution options for uploading your music to streaming platforms.

This app suits drummers who record their performances and want to make their tracks sound professional before sharing them online.

CHAPTER TEN
ACHIEVING MASTERY AND LIFELONG LEARNING

ARTIST SPOTLIGHT
GENE KRUPA

Gene Krupa was born on January 15, 1909, in Chicago, Illinois, and is widely regarded as one of the most influential drummers in jazz history. **Krupa** was a pioneering figure who brought the drums to the forefront of jazz ensembles, establishing the drum set as a solo instrument in its own right. His career spanned several decades, during which he continuously evolved his craft, becoming a key figure in modern drumming techniques and a significant influence on generations of drummers, including the legendary **Buddy Rich**.

Gene Krupa
Credit – Library of Congress via Picryl.com

Gene Krupa's journey into the world of jazz began in his childhood when his fascination with drums was already evident. By the time he was a teenager, he was making waves in the vibrant Chicago jazz scene, a testament to his prodigious talent. His dedication to his craft led him to study with respected teachers and play with numerous bands, where he began to shape his unique style. In 1927, he made the pivotal move to New York City and joined the **Benny Goodman Orchestra**, a step that would catapult him to fame for his energetic performances and innovative drumming techniques.

Krupa's career reached new heights in the late 1930s and 1940s, particularly with his famous solo on *"Sing, Sing, Sing"* with the **Benny Goodman Orchestra**, which became one of jazz's most iconic drum solos. He became known for his showmanship, power, and precision but continued learning and refining his craft. **Krupa** was constantly experimenting with new techniques and sounds, and he was one of the first drummers to use cymbals and tom-toms in a way that expanded the drum set's expressive possibilities.

Krupa was deeply committed to educating and mentoring young drummers throughout his career. He published instructional books, developed new drumsticks and equipment, and opened the *Gene Krupa Drum School* in New York. His passion for drumming matched his desire to share his knowledge with others, making him a beloved teacher and role model. **Krupa's** influence was particularly profound on **Buddy Rich**, who admired **Krupa's** technique and innovation. The two drummers developed close friendships and mutual respect, with **Krupa** praising **Rich's** extraordinary talent.

Gene Krupa's legacy as a drummer and educator continues to inspire musicians worldwide. His commitment to continuous learning, his willingness to experiment and innovate, and his dedication to teaching set a standard that many drummers have aspired to follow. **Krupa's** influence is not confined to his lifetime. Even after his passing on October 16, 1973, his impact on the world of drumming remains as strong as ever. **Gene Krupa** is a perfect example of the embodiment of mastery of the drums.

SECTION ONE
MASTERY THROUGH CONTINUOUS IMPROVEMENT
In this section, I will repeat a few concepts to emphasize their importance to drum mastery. Think of this as a recap, "bringing it all home."

IMPORTANCE OF DAILY PRACTICE
Consistent daily practice builds muscle memory and reinforces the technical skills needed to play complex rhythms and patterns. By practicing each day, drummers create a habit that ensures steady progress. Consistent practice helps refine techniques, master rudiments, and explore new styles, essential for versatility and growth as a drummer. This consistency also boosts confidence as progress becomes more tangible over time. Every musician experiences periods where progress seems to stall. Daily practice is vital to pushing through these plateaus.

By breaking down challenging sections, experimenting with different techniques, and gradually increasing the complexity of exercises, drummers can overcome these hurdles and continue their journey toward mastery.

EMBRACE CHALLENGES

To grow as a drummer, challenge yourself with complex pieces that require advanced techniques and nuanced playing, pushing you out of your comfort zone while fostering creativity and technical prowess. Ambitious goals drive continuous improvement.

Whether mastering a complex solo, performing a flawless live set, or exploring a new genre, setting high goals encourages drummers to strive for excellence. Analyzing what went wrong and understanding the root cause helps drummers avoid repeating the same errors.

This reflective practice fosters a growth mindset.

IMPORTANCE OF EAR TRAINING

Mastering the art of playing by ear will help you adapt to any performance situation, transforming you from a timekeeper to an expressive artist.

Honing your aural skills, understanding song structures, and conveying emotion through your performance will enrich the musical experience for you and your audience. Here are some ideas for ear training:

DYNAMIC CONTROL

As you listen to other drummers' techniques, concentrate on **Volume Variation:**

Ghost Notes: Incorporate softer strokes to add texture.

Accents: Emphasize specific beats to highlight rhythmic patterns.

ARTICULATION AND TOUCH

Practice emulating other drummers' **Stick Techniques:**

Moeller Method: Utilize wrist and arm motions for dynamic fluidity.

Surface Exploration:

Playing Zones: Strike different areas of the drum or cymbal to alter tone.

TEMPO FLEXABILITY

Listen to how other drummers handle the peaks and valleys of **Rubato Playing:**

Expressive Timing: Slightly speed up or slow down for emotional effect (use judiciously).

INTERPRETING MUSIC BY EAR TO CONTROL FEELINGS

EMOTIONAL AWARENESS

Understanding Context:

Song Meaning: Interpret the emotional message of the piece.

Personal Connection:

Internalize Emotions: Reflect on personal experiences to enhance expression.

MUSICAL EXPRESSION

Improvisation:

Emotive Solos: Create drum solos that tell a story or convey a mood.
Dynamic Shaping:
Crescendos and Decrescendos: Build or reduce intensity to mirror emotional arcs.

INTERACTION WITH OTHER MUSICIANS
Responsive Playing:
Musical Dialogue: Engage in a back-and-forth exchange with bandmates.
Supportive Role:
Enhancing Melodies: Use drumming to complement and elevate other instruments.

PRACTICAL EXERCISES FOR EAR TRAINING

DEVELOP AURAL SKILLS
Daily Listening Sessions:
Genre Exploration: Listen to unfamiliar styles to broaden rhythmic understanding.
Rhythm Reproduction:
Mimic Recordings: Try to replicate drum parts from songs by ear.

UNDERSTAND SONG STRUCTURES
Charting Songs:
Create Roadmaps: Write down song structures after listening to reinforce memory.
Genre Study:
Identify Patterns: Note common structural elements within specific genres.

FOCUS ON IMPORTANCE OF EXPRESSING EMOTION
Emotion-Focused Practice:
Mood Playing: Choose an emotion and attempt to express it through your drumming.
Feedback Loop:
Record and Review: Listen to your playing to assess emotional impact.

SEEK ADVANCED INSTRUCTION
Advanced teachers can provide personalized feedback, introduce new techniques, and offer insights that self-study might miss. They can also challenge drummers with exercises tailored to their skill level and goals. Workshops and masterclasses provide hands-on experience, direct interaction with experts, and the chance to observe advanced techniques in action. They also expose drummers to new styles, ideas, and approaches that can inspire and enhance their playing. In today's digital age, online courses provide access to a wealth of advanced drumming knowledge from the comfort of home.

These courses often include video tutorials, practice routines, and interactive feedback, allowing drummers to learn independently. Advanced online courses can cover topics like jazz drumming, complex polyrhythms, or studio recording techniques, offering tailored instruction to meet individual needs.

I WANT TO OFFER YOU A FREE GIFT

I hope you're loving this book so far. Learning an instrument can be daunting, but the rewards are exponential as you learn and grow your performance skills. I've created a list of **TEN SECRETS A MUSICIAN CANNOT LIVE WITHOUT,** and I want to share it with you.

If you want a free copy of my list, email us at...

<<   modernrenaissancepublishing@gmail.com   >>

with the subject line **TEN SECRETS FREE LIST,** and I'll email you back a free copy at no obligation whatsoever to you as a heartfelt thanks for reading this book.

AVOID STEREOTYPES

In all my music mastery books, I urge the reader to reject stereotypes. The most important thing you can do is what you don't do! Throughout my life, I've encountered people who bought into the negative stereotypes about musicians. When I mentioned that I was a musician, I would get a look from someone who immediately judged me as a loser. It's sad, but you will do all of us a favor if you exemplify yourself as a professional and never exhibit any of these negative stereotypes. My old friend, championship-winning *NFL* Quarterback, **Congressman and Secretary of Housing and Urban Development Jack Kemp** talked about it in a unique way. He said:

"Winning is like shaving – you do it every day or you wind up looking like a bum."

Tad Sisler with Congressman Jack Kemp
Source – Sisler Private Collection

It's all about the way you carry yourself, with pride and self-respect. People will pick up on your attitudes, emotions, and habits. Be the best version of yourself always and avoid these stereotypes:

MUSICIANS ARE UNRELIABLE AND IRRESPONSIBLE – People often stereotype musicians as flaky, unreliable, and irresponsible, particularly regarding commitments and punctuality. I will immediately write anyone off my call list who can't regularly show up on time with suitable instruments and clothing for the gig.

SUBSTANCE ABUSE – There is a pervasive stereotype that musicians are prone to drug and alcohol abuse, often glamorized in media and popular culture.

FINANCIAL INSTABILITY – Although this is something we cannot always control when we commit to this industry, unfortunately, many people stereotype musicians as struggling financially, living pay check to pay check, or unable to support themselves through their music alone. One of my friends who regularly comes to my gig has a running joke with me. He'll say, "You're good. Have you considered doing this for a living?" And I'll say, "No, it doesn't pay enough!" Everyone laughs, but the sad truth is that many musicians are grossly underpaid for their talents. But don't let this define you.

NO PRACTICAL SKILLS – Musicians are sometimes viewed as lacking practical or marketable skills outside of their music, contributing to the idea that they have few career options.

EGO AND ARROGANCE – Musicians, especially successful ones, are often stereotyped as having big egos or arrogant, believing they are superior because of their talent. I've worked with many excellent musicians who were impossible to work with. We sounded great on stage together, but the whole experience was not worth it because of their egos or negativity. Always try to enjoy the experience and let go!

UNCONVENTIONAL LIFESTYLE – There is a stereotype that musicians lead unconventional or chaotic lifestyles with irregular hours, frequent travel, and unstable relationships.

EMOTIONAL INSTABILITY – People sometimes judge as emotionally unstable or overly sensitive, with intense mood swings or dramatic behaviour.

PROMISCUITY – Particularly in rock and pop culture, musicians are often stereotyped as promiscuous and engaging in numerous short-term relationships. Groupies don't help erase this stereotype!

NON-CONFORMITY – People often see musicians as rebels or non-conformists who reject societal norms and conventional careers.

LACK OF FORMAL EDUCATION – There's a stereotype that musicians are less formally educated or lack academic achievements, focusing solely on their craft.

These stereotypes are not universally true and can be harmful, as they overlook many musicians' diversity, dedication, and professionalism. I must admit, though, that I've often told people I'm a composer, producer, author, entertainer, or many other titles (all true) besides musician. Help propel us all forward by going against the stereotype!

SECTION TWO
LIFELONG LEARNING

"Drumming is not just playing the drums; it's about feeling the music and expressing yourself through the beats." – Dave Weckl

Dave Weckl
Credit – Tore Saetre – Creativecommons.org

KEEP UP WITH NEW TRENDS
Several years ago, I was interviewed by a music blogger. She asked a hundred questions about production and composition, and then she had one last question, *"What would you consider your biggest challenge through your entire career?"* Instantly, I pointed out that keeping up with technology and staying current has been my biggest challenge. Technology is evolving at a pace we've never seen before, and to stay relevant you must stay current. My father-in-law was an excellent jazz pianist, but he stopped learning new things at some point in his life. Although he was a master performer, time eventually caught up with him, and his opportunities diminished. Not everyone is cut out to know all aspects of current technology, but you must always continue to learn and grow as much as you can to become a master.

Lifelong learning in music involves constantly broadening one's horizons by exploring new genres. For an advanced drummer, this could mean delving into unfamiliar styles such as Afro-Cuban rhythms, electronic music, or avant-garde jazz. This would expand your musical vocabulary, enhance your versatility, and help you stay inspired by fresh, diverse influences.

The music industry constantly evolves, with new technologies shaping how music is created, recorded, and performed. Advanced drummers should stay abreast of these changes, whether learning to use electronic drum kits, integrating digital effects, or mastering music production software. Adapting to technological advancements ensures that drummers remain relevant in an increasingly digital music landscape and can use innovative tools to enhance their artistry. Keep your ear to the ground as AI advances. Lifelong learning is fueled by a commitment to constant self-education. This involves seeking new resources, whether books, online courses, or video tutorials, to refine existing skills and learn new ones, studying advanced music theory, analyzing the work of other drummers, or exploring the history and cultural significance of different drumming traditions.

TEACHING AND SHARING KNOWLEDGE

Becoming a Music Mentor: Mentorship allows advanced drummers to share their expertise, offer guidance, and inspire the next generation. It's a rewarding way to reinforce one's own knowledge while making a positive impact on others.

Creating Instructional Content: Another way to share knowledge is by creating instructional content, such as books, online courses, or YouTube tutorials. Advanced drummers can leverage their experience to teach specific techniques, share practice routines, or break down complex concepts for learners at various levels.

Creating such content helps others and allows the drummer to solidify their understanding of the material and build a personal brand within the drumming community.

Participating in Music Education Programs: Formal music education programs allow advanced drummers to contribute to structured learning environments, interact with students, and collaborate with other educators. This experience enhances teaching skills and provides opportunities for professional networking and growth.

MUSIC COLLEGES/UNITED STATES:

Schools like the **Musicians Institute** in Hollywood, CA are completely acceptable. **MI** has an excellent vocal, drum, guitar, and audio engineering program. I have friends who work with headliner artists and compose for film and television who have graduated from **MI**. Here are some more prestigious schools of music education:

Juilliard School (New York, NY): **Juilliard** is renowned for its rigorous training and high standards, offering voice and opera performance degrees. Its alumni include **Renee Fleming, Nina Simone, Audra McDonald,** and **David Bryan.**

Berklee College of Music (Boston, MA): Known for its contemporary music programs, **Berklee offers** extensive vocal performance programs, including jazz and popular music. It has a diverse curriculum and notable alumni like **John Mayer** and **Esperanza Spalding**. This program has a high bar for qualification, so you should be excellent and prepared to be the best.

Curtis Institute of Music (Philadelphia, PA): **Curtis** is highly selective, admitting only a few students each year, and provides full-tuition scholarships to all its students. It focuses on classical and opera training with a strong emphasis on performance.

Indiana University Jacobs School of Music (Bloomington, IN): One of the largest music schools in the **United States, Jacobs** offers various programs and degrees in vocal performance. It has a notable faculty and alumni network, including **Joshua Bell** and **Leonard Slatkin.**

New England Conservatory of Music (Boston, MA): NEC offers comprehensive programs in voice and opera, with a strong emphasis on performance and musicianship. It is deeply integrated into **Boston's** vibrant music scene.

MUSIC COLLEGES/EUROPE:

Royal College of Music (London, UK): Founded in 1882, this institution is consistently ranked as one of the top music schools globally, offering a wide range of degrees in various musical disciplines and boasting top-notch facilities and a distinguished faculty.

Royal Conservatoire of Scotland (Glasgow, Scotland): Known for its excellent music, drama, and dance programs, the **Royal Conservatoire of Scotland** hosts over 500 public performances each year, providing ample performance opportunities for students.

Royal Academy of Music (London, UK): The oldest conservatoire in the **UK**, founded in 1822, the **Royal Academy of Music** offers a range of programs from Bachelor's Degrees to advanced diplomas. It has a rich history of producing celebrated musicians such as **Elton John** and **Annie Lennox.**

Conservatoire National Supérieur de Musique et de Danse de Paris (CNSMDP) (Paris, France): Established in 1795, **CNSMDP** is one of **Europe's** leading institutions for music and dance, with comprehensive programs in musical disciplines.

Universität für Musik und darstellende Kunst Wien (Vienna, Austria): Located in **Vienna**, a city renowned for its classical music heritage, this university offers many music degrees. It is one of the largest and most prestigious music schools in **Europe.**

Whatever you do, continually expand your horizons, and never stop learning. My biggest challenge in these times is keeping up with technological advances and staying current. Still, ultimately, making it all boils down to talent and persistence.

PERSONAL AND PROFESSIONAL GROWTH

Lifelong learning in music also involves continually setting new goals, both personal and professional. For an advanced drummer, this might mean mastering a challenging piece, composing original music, or collaborating on a high-profile project. Regular reflection on one's achievements is important for personal growth. Advanced drummers should take time to assess how far they've come, celebrate their successes, and identify areas for improvement. As drummers advance in their careers, balancing personal and professional life becomes increasingly important. This balance ensures that the pursuit of musical excellence doesn't come at the expense of personal well-being or relationships.

Maintaining this balance includes setting boundaries, scheduling time for non-musical activities, and prioritizing self-care. Achieving this balance allows drummers to sustain their passion for music over the long term while enjoying a fulfilling personal life.

"The ability to listen is one of the essential qualities of a great drummer."
— Jeff Porcaro

Jeff Porcaro
Credit – Wikimedia Commons

SECTION THREE
THE JOY OF MASTERY
CELEBRATING MILESTONES

The path to mastery in drumming is marked by numerous milestones, each representing a significant achievement in your journey. Embrace these accomplishments, whether they are mastering a complex rhythm, playing a challenging piece, or performing in front of an audience for the first time. Hosting recitals and performances provides a platform for sharing your passion with others. Recording your progress is another powerful way to see how far you've come, offering a tangible reminder of your growth and dedication over time.

MUSIC AS A LIFELONG PASSION

For many, drumming is not just a skill to be learned but a lifelong passion that brings profound joy and satisfaction. The therapeutic benefits of playing music cannot be overstated; it's a powerful way to relieve stress, clear the mind, and connect with one's emotions. Finding joy in daily practice is key to maintaining motivation and ensuring the learning process remains fulfilling rather than a chore. Beyond the technical aspects, drumming serves as a unique means of self-expression, allowing drummers to communicate emotions and stories through rhythm and sound, making every beat a personal statement.

FINAL THOUGHTS AND ENCOURAGEMENT

As you progress in your drumming journey, the greatest gift you can give yourself is believing in your potential. Every drummer, whether a beginner or advanced, can reach new heights with dedication and practice. Embrace all the challenges and triumphs in your journey. Remember, each step forward brings you one step closer to mastery. Stay committed, even when progress seems slow because consistency ultimately leads to success. Remember, drumming is not just about hitting the drums; it's about finding your rhythm in life, expressing yourself, and sharing that joy with others. Keep drumming, keep growing, and let your passion for music lead the way!

CONCLUSION

In this book, I've guided you through a comprehensive journey of mastering the art of drumming. I've emphasized the importance of mastering fundamental techniques, from basic rudiments to advanced drumming patterns, helping drummers build a strong technical foundation. Understanding rhythms has been a central theme, with detailed explanations of time signatures, syncopation, and groove, ensuring that readers grasp the essential timing and feel required to excel.

Throughout the book, I've highlighted the significance of enjoying the process, encouraging drummers to find joy in daily practice, and expressing themselves creatively through their instruments. Remember, the joy of drumming is what fuels your journey.

PERSISTENCE, PRACTICE, AND PASSION

The trio of persistence, practice, and passion is at the heart of drumming success. The book reinforces that consistent practice is the key to overcoming challenges, improving skills, and achieving drumming goals. The dedication to regular practice, even when progress feels slow, separates great drummers from the rest. Coupled with a passion for music, this persistence fuels growth, helping drummers push through obstacles and continue evolving as musicians.

YOUR CALL TO ACTION

As you finish this book, remember that your drumming journey is just that, a journey and not a destination. It's a continuous process of growth and learning. Set new goals, challenge yourself with more complex rhythms and techniques, and never stop learning.

Whether you're performing on stage, recording in the studio, or practicing at home, let your passion for drumming guide you. Stay committed, keep pushing your limits, and most importantly, enjoy every moment you spend behind the drum kit. The rhythm of your drumming journey continues—keep it alive, vibrant, and full of passion.

Thank you so much for embarking on this journey. I encourage you to share your progress and stories and never forget Albert Einstein's words: ***"Strive not to be a success, but rather to be of value."*** If you accomplish this feat, your success will be huge and rewarding.

PLEASE LEAVE A REVIEW

Now that you have everything you need to **excel in drums and percussion**, it's time to share your newfound knowledge and show other readers where they can find the same support.

Simply by leaving your honest opinion of this book on Amazon or wherever you purchased it, you'll help other **drummers** discover the information they're looking for and pass their passion for **playing music** forward.

Thank you for your help. The **passion for playing drums** is kept alive when we pass on our knowledge – and you're helping **me** to do just that.

If you purchased my book on Amazon, here's the link to leave your review:

https://www.amazon.com/review/review-your-purchases/?asin=1966258038

Or, you can just scan this QR code to get to the Amazon review page, and thanks!

GLOSSARY OF DRUMMING TERMS

A comprehensive glossary of terms commonly used by drummers to enhance understanding and communication within the craft.

A

- **Accent**: An emphasized note played louder or with more force than surrounding notes to create dynamic interest.
- **Acoustic Drums**: Traditional drums that produce sound acoustically without electronic amplification.
- **Afro-Cuban Rhythms**: Complex rhythms originating from African and Cuban music traditions, often featuring polyrhythms.
- **Alternate Stroke Roll**: A drumming rudiment where strokes alternate between hands in a continuous roll.
- **Ankles Technique**: Foot technique focusing on ankle movement for bass drum pedal control.

B

- **Backbeat**: The emphasis on beats two and four in 4/4 time, fundamental to rock and pop music.
- **Balance**: The even distribution of volume and tone between different drums and cymbals.
- **Bass Drum (Kick Drum)**: The largest drum in a kit, played with a foot pedal to produce low-pitched sounds.
- **Bell of the Cymbal**: The raised central area of a cymbal, producing a distinct, bright tone when struck.
- **Blast Beat**: A rapid drumming technique involving fast alternating strokes between the bass drum and snare.
- **Bounce**: The rebound of the drumstick off the drumhead, essential for speed and fluidity.
- **Brushes**: Drumstick alternatives with wire or nylon bristles used for softer, swishing sounds, often in jazz.

C

- **Cadence**: A rhythmic or melodic sequence signaling the end of a phrase or section.
- **Chops**: Slang for a drummer's technical proficiency and skill level.

- **Click Track**: A metronome-like audio track used during recording to maintain consistent tempo.
- **Closed Hi-Hat**: Position where the hi-hat cymbals are pressed together, producing a tight sound.
- **Cross-Stick (Rim Click)**: Technique where the stick is laid across the snare drum and struck against the rim.
- **Crash Cymbal**: A cymbal used for accenting beats, producing a loud, explosive sound.
- **Cymbal**: A concave metal plate producing sound when struck, essential for adding texture and accents.

D

- **Double Bass Drum**: Using two bass drums or a double pedal to play rapid bass drum patterns.
- **Double Paradiddle**: A rudiment consisting of a specific sticking pattern: RLRLRR or LRLRLL.
- **Drag**: A rudiment involving a rapid double stroke played before the main note.
- **Drumhead**: The membrane stretched over a drum shell, producing sound when struck.
- **Drum Kit (Drum Set)**: A collection of drums and cymbals arranged for playing by a single drummer.
- **Drumstick**: A stick used to strike drums and cymbals, typically made of wood like hickory or maple.
- **Dynamics**: Variations in loudness or intensity of playing, adding expression to music.

E

- **Electronic Drums**: Drum pads with sensors triggering electronic sounds, used for silent practice or unique sounds.
- **Endorsement**: A professional relationship where a drummer promotes a company's products.
- **Ergonomics**: The design of equipment and arrangement of components to optimize comfort and efficiency.

F

- **Fill**: A short, improvised passage used to bridge sections or add interest within a song.
- **Flam**: A rudiment where a grace note precedes the main stroke, creating a thicker sound.
- **Foot Pedal**: A device operated by the foot to play the bass drum or control the hi-hat cymbals.
- **Four-Way Coordination**: The ability to control both hands and feet independently while playing complex patterns.

G

- **Ghost Notes**: Very soft notes played between accented notes, adding subtlety to grooves.

- **Groove**: The overall feel or sense of swing in a rhythmic pattern that compels movement.
- **Grip**: The method of holding drumsticks, such as matched grip or traditional grip.

H

- **Half-Time Feel**: A rhythm where the tempo feels slowed down, often by halving the snare hits.
- **Hand Technique**: The methods and motions used to control sticks and produce different sounds.
- **Hi-Hat Cymbals**: Two cymbals mounted on a stand, opened and closed with a foot pedal, used for rhythm and texture.
- **Heel-Down Technique**: Bass drum pedal technique where the heel remains on the pedal plate for control.
- **Heel-Up Technique**: Technique where the heel is lifted off the pedal, allowing more power in strokes.

I

- **Independence**: The skill of controlling each limb separately to play different rhythms simultaneously.
- **In-The-Pocket**: Playing with a solid groove and timing that feels natural and locked with other musicians.

K

- **Kit**: Another term for the drum set or drum kit.
- **Kick Drum**: Slang for the bass drum.

L

- **Linear Drumming**: A style where no two limbs play at the same time, creating intricate rhythms.
- **Lug**: The hardware on a drum shell used to tighten the tension rods and adjust drumhead tension.

M

- **Matched Grip**: Holding both sticks in the same way, palms facing down, commonly used in modern drumming.
- **Metronome**: A device producing a steady beat to help musicians practice consistent timing.
- **Moeller Technique**: A method utilizing a whipping motion to produce power and speed efficiently.
- **Mute**: To dampen a drum or cymbal to reduce resonance and sustain.

N

- **Notation**: Written symbols representing musical rhythms and patterns for drums.

O

- **Offbeat**: The weaker beats in a measure, often emphasized in certain styles for rhythmic interest.
- **Odd Time Signature**: Time signatures that deviate from common counts, like 5/4 or 7/8.

P

- **Paradiddle**: A fundamental rudiment with the sticking pattern RLRR or LRLL, used for building dexterity.
- **Phrasing**: The way a drummer structures rhythms and fills within the context of a song.
- **Pocket**: See In-The-Pocket.
- **Polyrhythm**: The simultaneous use of two or more conflicting rhythms.
- **Practice Pad**: A portable, quiet surface used for practicing drumming techniques.

Q

- **Quarter Note**: A note value representing one beat in common time (4/4).

R

- **Rack Tom**: A medium-sized tom-tom mounted on a rack or stand above the bass drum.
- **Ratamacue**: A rudiment combining single strokes and drags.
- **Resonant Head**: The bottom drumhead on a tom or snare drum, affecting sustain and tone.
- **Ride Cymbal**: A large cymbal used to maintain a steady rhythmic pattern.
- **Rimshot**: A technique where the stick strikes the rim and head of the drum simultaneously.
- **Rudiments**: Basic patterns forming the foundation of drumming techniques.

S

- **Shell**: The body of the drum, typically made from wood, metal, or acrylic.
- **Shuffle**: A rhythm with a swung eighth-note feel, common in blues and jazz.
- **Snare Drum**: A drum with metal wires (snares) stretched across the bottom head, producing a sharp, crisp sound.
- **Stick Control**: Mastery over stick movements for precision and speed.
- **Subdivision**: Dividing beats into smaller rhythmic units, such as eighth notes or triplets.
- **Swing**: A rhythmic feel where notes are played with a slight delay, creating a groovy effect.

T

- **Tempo**: The speed at which music is played, measured in beats per minute (BPM).
- **Throne**: The seat a drummer uses, adjustable for height and comfort.
- **Time Signature**: Musical notation indicating how many beats are in each measure and what note value constitutes one beat.
- **Tom-Tom**: Cylindrical drums without snares, varying in size, used for fills and melodic drumming.
- **Traditional Grip**: Holding the stick in the non-dominant hand with an underhand grip, traditional in jazz.
- **Triplet**: Three notes played in the time of two, creating a swinging rhythm.

U

- **Upstroke**: The upward motion of the stick after striking, preparing for the next stroke and aiding in dynamics.

V

- **Vamp**: A repeating musical figure or accompaniment, often used as an introduction or background.
- **Velocity**: The speed and force with which a drum or cymbal is struck, affecting dynamics and tone.

W

- **Warm-Up**: Exercises performed before playing to prepare muscles and prevent injury.
- **Woodblock**: A small, wooden percussion instrument producing a sharp, hollow sound.

X

- **X-Hat**: An auxiliary hi-hat setup, often fixed in a closed or semi-open position for quick access.

Z

- **Zones (Drum/Cymbal Zones)**: Different areas on a drumhead or cymbal that produce varying tones when struck.

ABOUT THE AUTHOR

Tad Sisler is an American Composer, Author and Producer of feature films and music. More than a thousand of his original works are available through *iTunes, Amazon* and virtually every other major marketplace. Through the years, **Tad** created and released independent feature films and documentaries, television shows, developed a music store and vast collection of music for film and television usages, in addition to published screenplays and books. **Tad** is a voting member of *The Academy of Recording Arts & Sciences*. **Tad** invented a wireless karaoke all-in-one microphone that became a best-seller on *Amazon*. A child prodigy, Tad was playing advanced piano pieces at the age of 8, and rating superior in Classical piano competitions at 12. Tad won his first scholarship for singing at 12, attending the Idyllwild School of Music and the Arts, then affiliated with the University of Southern California.

FEATURE FILMS

Tad produced, edited, and released "**The Ghosts of Brewer Town**", a mystery feature film, currently available on *YouTube*.

TELEVISION PROJECTS

Tad launched the **Journey To An Extraordinary Life-Legends Among Us** documentary series, which chronicles the lives and careers of legendary artists, actors, sports figures and heroes of medicine, in a feature-film format.

BOOKS

Books, Audio Books and Podcasts released by Tad include "**Reflections in the Key of Life-The Steve Madaio Story**", chronicling the life and times of America's most prolific trumpeter. This book garnered a **Readers' Favorite Book Award** for Tad.

"**Mafia Baby**" is a shocking true story of a woman raped by a Mafioso, who then raised his child alone. Tad's autobiography, "**It's a Long Climb to The Middle**" *is* available currently on *Amazon* and *Barnes & Noble*. Screenplays in development by Tad Sisler include "**The Incredible Spark of Franklin Benjamin**", and "**Please Don't Forget**". Tad's latest **Music Mastery** collection of books is designed to educate and inspire musicians to become masters.

MUSIC

Tad's production music catalog tripled in size with the addition of thousands of excellent production music tracks, as well as hundreds of sound-alike tracks for the DJ/Karaoke industry, now distributed on **iTunes, Amazon Marketplace, CD Baby, Spotify, Rdio, Xbox Music** and dozens of other outlets Worldwide.

Tad produced and released "The Barcelona Sessions" to 1000 radio stations Worldwide, with never- before-heard original performances by Miles Davis' bassist, Bill Evan's drummer, Frank Sinatra's saxophonist, Maynard Ferguson's guitarist, and Andrae Crouch' flutist/saxophonist, produced by Tad Sisler in his recording studio.

Tad Sisler composed the full score to "**The Encore Of Tony Duran**", an indie feature film starring **Elliott Gould, William Katt, Nicki Ziering and Cody Kasch**, along with his co- composer Andrew Fraga, Jr. After having the distinction of being the first film to sell-out at the prestigious *Palm Springs International Film Festival*, the film won the **Jury Award** for **Best Feature Film** at the *Las Vegas Film Festival* and the *Santa Fe Film Festival*, as well as the **Indie Spirit Award** at the *Fort Lauderdale Film Festival* and the **Audience Favorite Award** at *Tallgrass Film Festival*, in conjunction with a **Lifetime Achievement Award** for **Elliott Gould**. The film is available on *Amazon Prime*.

Tad completed the music and audio editing for the TV Series "**American M.C.**". The first 7 episodes are complete and in the process of distribution through **iTunes**. Tad scored the Main Title theme to **American M.C.** as well as underscore and providing Music Supervision and source music.

PRODUCTION

Tad Sisler has been a valuable member of the team of specialists and project developers for **Yamaha Corporation of America**, delivering hundreds of intricate projects to exact **Yamaha** specifications over a 10 year period.

Tad received accolades in 2011 after being given the honor and challenge of doing the "official" remake of the iconic "**Andy Griffith Theme**" for the estate of the composer **Earle Hagen** as a perfect sound-alike, along with his composing associate Andrew Fraga, Jr.

Following a stint composing for a series entitled "**Famous Families**" on **Foxstar** and working as assistant to composer Jeff Edwards on the television series "**Silk Stalkings**" and "**Renegade**" in the late 1990's, Tad Sisler and founded & developed a production music catalog, containing thousands of high-quality music tracks available for sync licenses in film, television and advertising in more than 150 genres.

In addition to handling Music Supervision on "**The Encore Of Tony Duran**", and on "**American M.C.**", "**The Ghosts of Brewer Town**", "**Tis' The Season**", the "**Journey To an Extraordinary Life**" series, **Tad** produced the "**It's Everyone Else Who Has A Problem!**" series, and placed his original music on **NBC, ABC/Disney, Warner Brothers Television, TNT**, US National Infomercial campaigns through **Guthy/Renker** and **Script To Screen**, as well as custom composing for the TV and Advertising industry.

Tad released contains hundreds of top-quality soundalike tracks produced by **Tad** and his associates, for DJ and Karaoke usages, currently on *ITunes, Amazon Marketplace, Spotify, Rdio, Xbox Music,* and many other outlets.

LIVE PRODUCTION

In the 1980's and 1990's, **Tad** and his team produced a series of live headliner events at multiple venues from the ground up, including sold-out performances by **Kenny Rogers, Earth, Wind & Fire, Los Lobos, Glen Campbell, The Righteous Brothers, Lou Rawls, Tito Puente,** the **Power Jam** featuring **Timmy T, Tara Kemp, Candyman, Soul To Soul** and more.

HISTORY

As a very young man, Tad Sisler worked as a performer for **Frank Sinatra**, studied music in choreography under world-famous Broadway Dancer/Choreographer **Jacque D'Amboise**, received superior ratings in classical piano performance in tough **Joanna Hodges** international competitions, and received private acting lessons from **Richard Burton**, a friend of his family.

Tad attended the prestigious **Idyllwild School of Music and the Arts** on vocal music scholarships during the period when it was affiliated with the **University of Southern California**. In High School, Tad was one of 100 statewide vocalists elected to the prestigious **All-State Choir** in Missouri.

During his storied career, Tad has also had the honor of performing with and working among such greats as **Gladys Knight, Rita Coolidge, B.B. King, Marilyn McCoo, Johnny Mathis, Kenny Rogers, Tito Puente, Sonny and Mary Bono, Gene Barry, Teri Cole Whittaker, Shecky Greene, Peter Marshall, Mary Hart, Blackwell, Herb Jeffries, Trini Lopez, Glen Campbell, Jennifer Hudson** and other legends.

Tad Sisler's extensive experience, state of the art facility and history of delivering quality feature films and music on time and on budget, as well as the ability to draw from an extensive catalog of production music, allows his experienced team to offer complete services in custom film and television production as well as in music composition and production efficiently.

Tad is proud and humbled to be a voting member of the **Academy of Recording Arts & Sciences**, which allows him to have a voice to vote for great artists worthy of winning a **Grammy Award**. Many of Tad's works have been placed into Grammy consideration.

In 2023, Tad won a prestigious **Telly Award** for creative excellence in his *Journey to an Extraordinary Life* film series.

Modern Renaissance Publishing is at the forefront of a new intellectual awakening, dedicated to fostering a renaissance of ideas that resonate in today's world.

Our mission is to bring cutting-edge concepts and timeless wisdom to the public through a diverse array of publishing formats, including books, eBooks, and audiobooks. We are proud to launch our **Music Mastery** series, offering comprehensive guides and insights for musicians of all levels.

In addition to our literary endeavors, we also publish original music, enriching the cultural landscape with creative expressions. Whether you're seeking to expand your knowledge, enhance your skills, or simply be inspired,

Modern Renaissance Publishing provides the resources and content to empower your journey. Join us as we bridge the rich heritage of the past with the innovative spirit of the present to shape a brighter, more enlightened future.

REFERENCES

License link to all Wikimedia Commons and Creative Commons photo credit references: Creative Commons. (n.d.). *Attribution-ShareAlike 4.0 International (CC BY-SA 4.0)* [License]. Retrieved from https://creativecommons.org/licenses/by-sa/4.0/

BrainyQuote. (n.d.). *Top 10 Ringo Starr quotes.* https://www.brainyquote.com/lists/authors/top-10-ringo-starr-quotes

ElephantDrums. (n.d.). *Famous drummers and their inspirational drumming quotes.* https://www.elephantdrums.co.uk/blog/guides-and-resources/drumming-quotes-famous-drummers/

AZQuotes. (n.d.). *Drumsticks quotes.* https://www.azquotes.com/quotes/topics/drumsticks.html

AZQuotes. (n.d.). *Cymbals quotes.* https://www.azquotes.com/quotes/topics/cymbals.html

Wax, M. (2012, June). *Marty Morell on Bill Evans, pt. 1.* JazzWax. https://www.jazzwax.com/2012/06/marty-morell-on-bill-evans-pt-1.html

AZQuotes. (n.d.). *Drumming quotes.* https://www.azquotes.com/quotes/topics/drumming.html

BrainyQuote. (n.d.). *Rod Stewart quotes.* https://www.brainyquote.com/search_results?x=0&y=0&q=ROD+STEWART

uDiscoverMusic. (n.d.). *Glen Campbell: 20 quotes.* https://www.udiscovermusic.com/stories/glen-campbell-20-quotes/

BrainyQuote. (n.d.). *Stevie Wonder quotes.* https://www.brainyquote.com/authors/stevie-wonder-quotes

BrainyQuote. (n.d.). *Improvisation quotes.* https://www.brainyquote.com/search_results?x=0&y=0&q=improvisation

Drumeo. (2019, July 15). *The great Steve Gadd: Are you paying bills or bringing thrills with your playing?* [Facebook post]. https://www.facebook.com/drumeo/posts/the-great-steve-gadd-are-you-paying-bills-or-bringing-thrills-with-your-playing-/2377097262389871/

Drumeo. (n.d.). *John Bonham: Drum genius.* https://www.drumeo.com/beat/john-bonham-drum-genius/

DrumSpy. (n.d.). *Famous drumming quotes.* https://drumspy.com/famous-drumming-quotes/

BrainyQuote. (n.d.). *Drummer quotes.* https://www.brainyquote.com/topics/drummer-quotes

QuoteFancy. (n.d.). *Khloe Kardashian quotes.*
https://quotefancy.com/khloe-kardashian-quotes

IMDb. (n.d.). *Larry King quotes.*
https://www.imdb.com/name/nm0420370/quotes/?ref_=nm_dyk_qu

Facts.net. (n.d.). *20 captivating facts about Sergio Mendes.*
https://facts.net/celebrity/20-captivating-facts-about-sergio-mendes/

BrainyQuote. (n.d.). *Fatigue quotes.*
https://www.brainyquote.com/search_results?q=fatigue&pg=3

BrainyQuote. (n.d.). *Learning quotes.*
https://www.brainyquote.com/search_results?x=0&y=0&q=LEARNING

BrainyQuote. (n.d.). *Creativity quotes.*
https://www.brainyquote.com/search_results?x=0&y=0&q=creativity

BrainyQuote. (n.d.). *Fulfillment quotes.*
https://www.brainyquote.com/search_results?q=fulfillment&pg=3

BrainyQuote. (n.d.). *Junior Seau quotes.*
https://www.brainyquote.com/search_results?x=0&y=0&q=junior+seau

BrainyQuote. (n.d.). *Larry King quotes.*
https://www.brainyquote.com/search_results?x=0&y=0&q=larry+king

BrainyQuote. (n.d.). *Criticism quotes.*
https://www.brainyquote.com/search_results?x=0&y=0&q=CRITICISM

PositiveQuotes. (n.d.). *34 inspirational drum quotes.*
https://positivequotes.web.2nt.com/morigan/34-inspirational-drum-quotes.html

BrainyQuote. (n.d.). *Success quotes.*
https://www.brainyquote.com/search_results?x=0&y=0&q=success

The Drum Rudiments. (n.d.). *Books archives.*
https://thedrumrudiments.com/category/books/

BrainyQuote. (n.d.). *Interaction quotes.*
https://www.brainyquote.com/search_results?q=interaction&pg=2

Ruiz, M. (n.d.). *The four agreements.* https://www.miguelruiz.com/the-four-agreements

BrainyQuote. (n.d.). *Visualization quotes.*
https://www.brainyquote.com/search_results?x=0&y=0&q=VISUALIZATION

BrainyQuote. (n.d.). *Percussion quotes.*
https://www.brainyquote.com/search_results?x=0&y=0&q=percussion

IdolBirthdays. (n.d.). *Gene Krupa - Age, bio, faces and birthday.*
https://www.idolbirthdays.net/gene-krupa

Bookroo. (n.d.). *Learning quotes.* https://bookroo.com/quotes/learning

YouTube. (2023). *[Journey To an Extraordinary Life-Tad Sisler and Louie Stevens]*. YouTube. **https://www.youtube.com/watch?v=-wYCSRDyIic**

ScienceDaily. (2024, January 29). *Playing an instrument boosts brain's executive function, study finds*. ScienceDaily. **https://www.sciencedaily.com/releases/2024/01/240129122415.htm**

AZ Quotes. (n.d.). *Elliott Gould quotes*. AZ Quotes. **https://www.azquotes.com/author/31289-Elliott_Gould**

Orthopedic Specialists of SW Florida. (n.d.). *Ergonomic tips for office workers: Preventing hand, wrist & elbow strain*. **https://www.osswf.com/blog/ergonomic-tips-for-office-workers-preventing-hand-wrist-elbow-strain**

MODERN RENAISSANCE
PUBLISHING